IB

Chemistry (SL and HL) Examination

SECRETS

Study Guide
Your Key to Exam Success

IB Test Review for the
International Baccalaureate
Diploma Programme

Dear Future Exam Success Story:

Congratulations on your purchase of our study guide. Our goal in writing our study guide was to cover the content on the test, as well as provide insight into typical test taking mistakes and how to overcome them.

Standardized tests are a key component of being successful, which only increases the importance of doing well in the high-pressure high-stakes environment of test day. How well you do on this test will have a significant impact on your future, and we have the research and practical advice to help you execute on test day.

The product you're reading now is designed to exploit weaknesses in the test itself, and help you avoid the most common errors test takers frequently make.

How to use this study guide

We don't want to waste your time. Our study guide is fast-paced and fluff-free. We suggest going through it a number of times, as repetition is an important part of learning new information and concepts.

First, read through the study guide completely to get a feel for the content and organization. Read the general success strategies first, and then proceed to the content sections. Each tip has been carefully selected for its effectiveness.

Second, read through the study guide again, and take notes in the margins and highlight those sections where you may have a particular weakness.

Finally, bring the manual with you on test day and study it before the exam begins.

Your success is our success

We would be delighted to hear about your success. Send us an email and tell us your story. Thanks for your business and we wish you continued success.

Sincerely,

Mometrix Test Preparation Team

Need more help? Check out our flashcards at: http://MometrixFlashcards.com/IB

TABLE OF CONTENTS

Top 20 Test Taking Tips

1. Carefully follow all the test registration procedures
2. Know the test directions, duration, topics, question types, how many questions
3. Setup a flexible study schedule at least 3-4 weeks before test day
4. Study during the time of day you are most alert, relaxed, and stress free
5. Maximize your learning style; visual learner use visual study aids, auditory learner use auditory study aids
6. Focus on your weakest knowledge base
7. Find a study partner to review with and help clarify questions
8. Practice, practice, practice
9. Get a good night's sleep; don't try to cram the night before the test
10. Eat a well balanced meal
11. Know the exact physical location of the testing site; drive the route to the site prior to test day
12. Bring a set of ear plugs; the testing center could be noisy
13. Wear comfortable, loose fitting, layered clothing to the testing center; prepare for it to be either cold or hot during the test
14. Bring at least 2 current forms of ID to the testing center
15. Arrive to the test early; be prepared to wait and be patient
16. Eliminate the obviously wrong answer choices, then guess the first remaining choice
17. Pace yourself; don't rush, but keep working and move on if you get stuck
18. Maintain a positive attitude even if the test is going poorly
19. Keep your first answer unless you are positive it is wrong
20. Check your work, don't make a careless mistake

Stoichiometric Relationships

Kinetic Molecular Theory and Ideal Gas Laws

Kinetic molecular theory

The kinetic molecular theory consists of several assumptions including the following:
1. Ideal gas molecules are in constant random motion. The gas molecules travel in straight lines until they collide with other gas molecules or with the walls of the container.
2. Ideal gas molecules have a negligible volume compared to the volume of the gas itself. Most of the volume of a gas is empty space.
3. Ideal gas molecules exert no attractive or repulsive forces on each other.
4. Ideal gas molecules have a kinetic energy that is directly proportional to the absolute temperature. The higher the temperature, the higher the average kinetic energy of the gas molecules, and the faster the gas molecules are moving.
5. Ideal gas molecules have perfectly elastic collisions. The kinetic energy lost by one gas molecule is gained by another gas molecule. No energy is lost in the collision with the container.

Ideal gases

An ideal gas is a hypothetical or theoretical gas. Ideal gases are assumed to be a set of randomly moving point particles that do not interact with each other. The collisions of ideal gases are assumed to be completely elastic, and the intermolecular forces are assumed to be zero. Real gases show more complex behaviors. The ideal gas laws tend to fail at low temperatures and high pressures when the effects of the particle size and intermolecular forces are more apparent. Also, the idea gas assumptions do not account for phase transitions.

Avogadro's law

Avogadro's law describes the relationship between the volume and amount in moles of an ideal gas at a constant pressure and temperature. For an ideal gas, the volume and the number of moles are directly related. If the volume increases, the number of moles would have to increase in order to maintain the pressure and temperature. If the number of moles in the container increases, the volume will also need to increase to maintain the same pressure and temperature. The relationship between volume and amount in mole of a gas is represented by $V \propto N, V = kN$, or $\frac{V}{N} = k$. Because the quotient of the volume and the amount in moles is a constant, Avogadro's law can be stated as $\frac{V_i}{N_i} = \frac{V_f}{N_f}$.

Boyle's law

Boyle's law describes the relationship between the volume and pressure of an ideal gas at a constant temperature for a given amount of gas. For an ideal gas, volume and pressure are inversely related. Because gases are compressible, if the pressure of a gas sample is increased, the volume will decrease. If the pressure of a gas sample is decreased, the volume will increase. Conversely, if the volume of a gas sample is increased, the pressure will decrease. If the volume of a gas sample is decreased, the pressure will increase. For example, if the pressure of a gas sample is doubled, the volume decreases to one-half of the original volume. If the pressure of a gas sample is tripled, the volume decreases to one-third of the original volume. The relationship between volume and pressure is represented by $V \propto \frac{1}{P}$ or $V = k\frac{1}{P}$ or $PV = k$. Because the product of the pressure and the volume is a constant, Boyle's law can be stated as $P_i V_i = P_f V_f$.

Charles's law

Charles's law describes the relationship between the volume and temperature of an ideal gas at a constant pressure for a given amount of gas. For an ideal gas, volume and temperature are directly related. Because the kinetic energy of a gas is directly proportional to the absolute temperature, if the temperature increases, the average kinetic energy of the gas molecules increases. As the molecules move faster, they will spread farther apart as long as the pressure remains constant, which increases the volume. If the volume of the container were to increase, the temperature would also have to increase if it were to maintain a constant pressure, since the molecules must move faster to strike the container as often. The relationship between volume and pressure is represented by $V \propto T$ or $V = kT$ or $\frac{V}{T} = k$. Because the quotient of the volume and the temperature is a constant, Charles's law can be stated as $\frac{V_i}{T_i} = \frac{V_f}{T_f}$, where the temperature is stated in kelvin.

Combined gas law

The combined gas law combines Boyle's law and Charles's law. According to Boyle's law, volume and pressure are inversely related, or $V \propto \frac{1}{P}$. According to Charles's law, volume and temperature are directly related, or $V \propto T$. Combining these relationships into one yields $V \propto \frac{T}{P}$ or $V = k\frac{T}{P}$.
Solving for k yields $\frac{PV}{T}$. Because $k = \frac{P_1 V_1}{T_1}$ and $k = \frac{P_2 V_2}{T_2}$, the combined gas law can be written as $\frac{P_1 V_1}{T_1} = \frac{P_2 V_2}{T_2}$. For situations in which $V_1 = V_2$, the combined gas law yields a relationship of $P \propto T$, indicating that for a constant volume, the pressure and temperature are directly related.

Ideal gas law

The ideal gas law combines Boyle's law, Charles's law, and Avogadro's law. According to Boyle's law, $V \propto \frac{1}{P}$. According to Charles's law, $V \propto T$. According to Avogadro's law, $V \propto n$. Combining these three relationships into one relationship yields $V \propto \frac{nT}{P}$. Multiplying through by P yields $PV \propto nT$, or $PV = nRT$, where R is the ideal gas constant of 0.0821 L·atm/(K·mol), P is the pressure in atm, V is the volume in L, n is the number of moles in mol, and T is the temperature in K.

Real gases

Although assuming that gases are ideal is appropriate for many situations, real gases behave differently than ideal gases. The collisions of real gases are not elastic. Real gases do have attractive and repulsive forces. Real gases have mass, whereas ideal gases do not. The atoms or molecules of real gases are not point particles, and they do interact with each other especially under high pressures and low temperatures. Under the right conditions of pressure and temperature, real gases will undergo phase transitions and become liquids. The pressure of real gases is less than those of ideal gases due to the small attractive forces between the particles in the gases.

Problem #1

A 5.0 L gas sample has a pressure of 1.0 standard atmosphere (atm). If the pressure is increased to 2.0 atm, find the new volume. Assume that the temperature is constant.

To find the new volume, use the equation associated with Boyle's law $P_i V_i = P_f V_f$. Solving the equation for the unknown V_f yields $V_f = \frac{P_i V_i}{P_f}$. Substituting in the given values $P_i = 1.0$ atm, $V_i = 5.0$ L, and $P_f = 2.0$ atm into the equation yields $V_f = \frac{(1.0 \text{ atm})(5.0 \text{ L})}{(2.0 \text{ atm})} = 2.5$ L. This checks because the pressure increased and the volume decreased. More specifically, because the pressure was doubled, the volume was reduced to one-half of the original volume.

Problem #2

A gas sample has a volume of 10.0 L at 200.0 K. Find its volume if the temperature is increased to 300.0 K.

To find the new volume, use the equation associated with Charles's law $\frac{V_i}{T_i} = \frac{V_f}{T_f}$. Solving the equation for the unknown V_f yields $V_f = \frac{T_f V_i}{T_i}$. Substituting the given values $V_i = 10.0$ L, $T_i = 200.0$ K, and $T_f = 300.0$ K into the equation yields $V_f = \frac{(300.0 \text{ K})(10.0 \text{ L})}{(200.0 \text{ K})} = 15.0$ L. This checks because the temperature increased and the volume increased. Also, note that if the temperature had not been stated in kelvin, it would have to be converted to kelvin before substituting the values in to the equation.

<u>Problem #3</u>

Find the pressure that 0.500 mol of H_2 (g) will exert on a 500.0 mL flask at 300.0 K.

To calculate the pressure that 0.500 mol of H_2 will exert on a 500.0 mL flask at 300.0 K, use the ideal gas equation $PV = nRT$, where R is the ideal gas constant of 0.0821 L·atm/(K·mol), P is the pressure in atm, V is the volume in L, n is the number of moles in mol, and T is the temperature in kelvin. Solving the ideal gas equation for P yields $P = \frac{nRT}{V}$. First, convert the 500.0 mL to 0.500 L. Substituting in n = 0.500 mol, V = 0.500 L, T = 300.0 K, and $R = 0.0821 \frac{\text{L·atm}}{\text{K·mol}}$ yields $P = \frac{(0.500 \text{ mol})(0.0821 \text{ L·atm/(K·mol)})(300.0 \text{ K})}{(0.500 \text{ L})} = 24.6$ atm.

Naming Simple Inorganic Compounds

Naming process for binary molecular compounds

The names of binary molecular compounds follow this pattern:
- prefix + first element name (space) prefix + root of second element name + -ide.

If a prefix ends with *a* or *o* and the element name begins with *a* or *o*, the first *a* or *o* of the prefix is dropped. For example, N_2O_5 is named dinitrogen pentoxide. The prefix *mono-* is usually dropped unless more than one binary compound may be formed from the two elements involved.

Binary Molecular Compounds			
#	Prefix	#	Prefix
1	mono-	6	hexa-
2	di-	7	hepta-
3	tri-	8	octa-
4	tetra-	9	nona-
5	penta-	10	deca-

Naming process for binary ionic compounds

The names of binary ionic compounds follow this pattern:
- cation name (space) anion name.

The name of simple cations is usually the element name. For example, the K^+ cation is named potassium. Some cations exist in more than one form. In those cases, the charge of the ion follows the element as a Roman numeral in parentheses. For example, the Cu^+ ion is named copper(I) and the Cu^{2+} ion is named copper(II). Simple anions are named with the root of the element name followed by the suffix -*ide*. For example, the O^{2-} anion is named oxide, and the F^- ion is named fluoride. The following are some examples of names of binary ionic compounds: KI is named potassium iodide, and FeO is named iron(II) oxide.

<u>Examples</u>

N_2O_4 — This is a binary molecular compound. Using the prefixes *di-* for 2 and *tetra-* for 4, this compound is named dinitrogen tetroxide. Note that the entire element name is retained for the cation, but the root plus *-ide* is used for the anion name.

S_2F_{10} — This is a binary molecular compound. Using the prefixes *di-* for 2 and *deca-* for 10, this compound is named disulfur decafluoride. Note that the entire element name is retained for the cation, but the root plus *-ide* is used for the anion name.

Fe_2O_3 — This is a binary ionic compound. Iron forms two types of cations Fe^{2+} and Fe^{3+}, but because the anion is O^{2-}, this must be the Fe^{3+} ion in order to balance the charges. This compound is named iron(III) oxide.

$CuCl_2$ — This is a binary ionic compound. Copper forms two types of cations Cu^+ and Cu^{2+}, but because the anion is Cl^-, this must be the Cu^{2+} ion in order to balance the charges. This compound is named copper(II) chloride.

Naming acids

Acids are generally categorized as binary acids or oxyacids. Binary acids are named by the pattern: *hydro-* + root of element + *-ic* (space) acid. For example, HI is named hydroiodic acid, and HCl is named hydrochloric acid. One exception is that in hydrosulfuric acid (H_2S), the entire element name sulfur is used. The names of oxyacids depend on the endings of their polyatomic anions. If the polyatomic anions end in *-ate*, then the acid names end in *-ic*. If the anions end in *-ite*, the acid names end in *-ous*. The naming pattern for an oxyacid is as follows: anion root + ending (space) acid. For example, H_2CO_3 is named carbonic acid because the carbonate ion ends in *-ate*, and H_2SO_3 is named sulfurous acid because the sulfite ion ends in *-ite.*

Naming hydrates

Hydrates form from salts (ionic compounds) that attract water. Hydrates are named from their salt (ionic compound) name and the number of water molecules involved in the following pattern:
salt name (space) prefix + hydrate.

For example, the name of $CuSO_4 \cdot 5H_2O$ is copper(II) sulfate pentahydrate, and the name of $CoCl_2 \cdot 6H_2O$ is cobalt(II) chloride hexahydrate.

Binary Molecular Compounds			
#	Prefix	#	Prefix
1	mono-	6	hexa-
2	di-	7	hepta-
3	tri-	8	octa-
4	tetra-	9	nona-
5	penta-	10	deca-

Naming bases and salts

Bases typically are ionic compounds with the hydroxide anion and are named following the conventions of naming ionic compounds. For example, NaOH is named sodium hydroxide and $Mg(OH)_2$ is named magnesium hydroxide. Salts are ionic compounds with any cation except H^+ from an aqueous base and any anion except OH^- from an aqueous acid. Salts are named like regular ionic compounds with the name of the cation followed by the name of the anion. Examples of salts include sodium chloride (NaCl), potassium fluoride (KF), magnesium iodide (MgI_2), $NaC_2H_5O_2$ (sodium acetate), and ammonium carbonate (($NH_4)_2CO_3$).

Naming Common Organic Compounds

Naming alkanes, alkenes, and alkynes

Hydrocarbons may be classified as alkanes, alkenes, and alkynes based on the type of covalent bonds between the carbon atoms. Molecules with only single bonds between carbon atoms are called alkanes with names ending in -*ane*. Molecules with at least one double bond between carbon atoms are called alkenes with names ending in -*ene*. Molecules with at least one triple bond between carbon atoms are called alkynes with names ending in -*yne*. The prefixes of alkanes, alkenes, alkynes are based on the number of carbon atoms. These prefixes are given by the table below. For example, an alkane with one carbon atom would be named methane. An alkane with two carbon atoms would be named ethane. An alkene with two carbon atoms would be named ethene. An alkene with five carbon atoms would be named pentene. An alkyne with four carbon atoms would be named butyne. An alkyne with eight carbon atoms would be named octyne.

Hydrocarbons			
#	Prefix	#	Prefix
1	meth-	6	hexa-
2	eth-	7	hepta-
3	prop-	8	octa-
4	but-	9	nona-
5	penta-	10	deca-

Naming alcohols, ethers, ketones, aldehydes, and amines

To name an alcohol, drop the -*e* from the name of the hydrocarbon and add -*ol.* For example, when the functional group for an alcohol replaces one hydrogen in methane, then the name is changed to methanol. Likewise, ethane becomes ethanol.

Ethers are named for the two hydrocarbons that flank the functional group. The root of the shorter of the two chains is named first. This is followed by -*oxy-*, which is then followed by the name of the longer chain. For example, $CH_3OCH_2CH_3$ is named methoxyethane.

To name a ketone, drop -*e* from the name of the hydrocarbon and add -*one.* For example, when the functional group for a ketone is inserted into propane, the name is changed to propanone, which is commonly known as acetone.

- 7 -

To name an aldehyde, drop the -e from the name of the hydrocarbon and add -al. For example, when the functional group for an aldehyde is substituted into methane, the aldehyde name would be methanal.

Amines may be named in more than one way. The two most common ways are either with the prefix amino- or the suffix -amine. Two simple amines are methylamine (CH_3NH_2) and ethylamine ($CH_3CH_2NH_2$).

Mole Concept

Avogadro's number, molar mass, and the mole

Avogadro's number is equivalent to the number of atoms in 12 g of the carbon-12 isotope or the number of atoms in 1 mole of carbon-12. Avogadro's number is numerically equal to approximately 6.022×10^{23}. Just like a dozen eggs represents 12 eggs and a pair of shoes represents 2 shoes, Avogadro's number of atoms represents 6.022×10^{23} atoms. *Molar mass* is the mass of one mole of a substance in grams. The *mole* is Avogadro's number of anything. For example, 1 mole of carbon atoms is 6.022×10^{23} carbon atoms, and 1 mole of CCl_4 contains 6.022×10^{23} molecules of CCl_4.

Problem #1

Determine the mass of 2.50 moles of O_2. (The atomic mass of oxygen is 16.0 u.)

To convert from moles of O_2 to mass in grams of O_2, use the dimensional analysis method with the molar mass of O_2. The molar mass of O_2 is 2(16.0 g) or 32.0 g. This molar mass can be written as the conversion factor $\left(\frac{32.0 \text{ g } O_2}{\text{mol } O_2}\right)$. Then, using dimensional analysis, multiply (2.50 mol O_2)$\left(\frac{32.0 \text{ g } O_2}{\text{mol } O_2}\right)$. The "mol O_2" cancels from the numerator of the first factor and the denominator of the second factor resulting in 80.0 g O_2.

Problem #2

Determine the number of moles of 100.0 g of $C_{12}H_{22}O_{11}$. (The atomic masses of C, H, and O are 12.0 u, 1.0 u, and 16.0 u, respectively.)

To find the number of moles of a sample of $C_{12}H_{22}O_{11}$, first, calculate the molar mass to be used in dimensional analysis. The molar mass of $C_{12}H_{22}O_{11}$ = 12(12.0 g) + 22(1.0 g) + 11(16.0 g) = 144.0 g + 22.0 g + 176.0 g = 342 g. This means that every mole of $C_{12}H_{22}O_{11}$ has a molar mass of 342 g. To convert from grams to moles, use dimensional analysis as follows: $(100.0 \text{ g } C_{12}H_{22}O_{11}) \left(\frac{1 \text{ mol } C_{12}H_{22}O_{11}}{342 \text{ g}}\right) = 0.292$ mol.

<u>Problem #3</u>

Given the reaction $3H_2(g) + N_2(g) \rightarrow 2NH_3(g)$, explain how to determine how many grams of nitrogen gas are needed to produce 100.0 g of ammonia. (The molar mass of N_2 = 28.0 g; the molar mass of NH_3 = 17.0 g.)

One approach to working out this problem is to use the dimensional analysis method all the way through the work of the problem. Conversion factors using the molar masses of NH_3 and N_2 are used as well as a mole ratio from the balanced chemical equation. The approach is to convert from grams of NH_3 to moles of NH_3, then to convert moles of NH_3 to moles of N_2, and finally to convert the moles of N_2 to grams of N_2.

$$\left(\frac{100.0 \text{ g } NH_3}{1}\right)\left(\frac{1 \text{ mol } NH_3}{17.0 \text{ g}}\right)\left(\frac{1 \text{ mol } N_2}{2 \text{ mol } NH_3}\right)\left(\frac{28.0 \text{ g } N_2}{1 \text{ mol } N_2}\right) = 82.4 \text{ g } N_2.$$

Calculating an empirical formula and a molecular formula of a compound

To find the empirical formula of a compound, first, calculate the masses of each element in the compound based on the percent composition that is given. Then, convert these masses to moles by dividing by the molar masses of those elements. Next, divide these amounts in moles by the smallest calculated value in moles and round to the nearest tenth. These calculations provide the subscripts for each element in the empirical formula. To find the molecular formula, divide the actual molar mass of the compound by the molar mass of the empirical formula.

<u>Example</u>

Find the empirical formula and the molecular formula for hydrogen peroxide given that it has a composition of 5.94 % hydrogen and 94.1 % oxygen. (The atomic mass for hydrogen = 1.008 u; the atomic mass of oxygen = 16.00 u.)

To find the empirical formula, calculate the masses of each element in hydrogen peroxide for a sample size of 100.0 g. Calculating 5.94 % of 100.0 g yields 5.94 g of hydrogen. Calculating 94.1 % of 100.0 g yields 94.1 g of oxygen. Next, convert the masses of these elements to moles. Multiplying $(5.94 \text{ g hydrogen}) \left(\frac{\text{mol hydrogen}}{1.008 \text{ g}}\right) = 5.89$ mol hydrogen. Multiplying $(94.1 \text{ g oxygen}) \left(\frac{\text{mol oxygen}}{16.00 \text{ g}}\right) = 5.88$ mol oxygen. Now, divide these amounts by the smallest value of moles that was calculated and round to the nearest tenth. For hydrogen, $\left(\frac{5.89}{5.88}\right) = 1.0$, and for oxygen, $\left(\frac{5.88}{5.88}\right) = 1.0$. These calculations are the subscripts for the empirical formula. Therefore, the empirical formula of hydrogen peroxide is HO. To find the molecular formula, find the molar mass of the empirical formula (HO) by adding 1.008 g + 16.00 g = 17.008 g. To perform the calculation, the molar mass of hydrogen peroxide would need to be given. If the problem states that the actual molar mass of hydrogen peroxide is 34.016 g, divide this molar mass by the molar mass of the empirical formula: $\frac{34.016}{17.008} = 2$. Multiply each subscript of the empirical formula by 2. The molecular formula for hydrogen peroxide is H_2O_2.

Calculating percent composition when given the molecular formula

To find the percent composition when given the molecular formula, first find the molar mass of the compound. Next, find the percent contributed by each element of the compound by dividing the molar mass of the element (remembering to multiply through by the subscripts of the molecular formula) by the molar mass of the compound. Finally, check the calculations by totaling these individual percents of the elements to ensure their combined total is 100 %. This may be slightly off if any of the numbers used were rounded.

<u>Example</u>

Find the percent composition of methane (CH_4). (The atomic mass of carbon = 12.01 u; the atomic mass of hydrogen = 1.008 u.)

To find the percent composition of methane, first find the molar mass of methane. The molar mass of methane is given by 12.01 g + 4(1.008 g) = 16.042 g. Next, find the percent contributed by the carbon and the percent contributed by the hydrogen. For the carbon, % C = $\frac{12.01 \text{ g/mol}}{16.042 \text{ g/mol}} \times 100\% =$ 74.87 %. For the hydrogen, % H = $\frac{4(1.008) \text{ g/mol}}{16.042 \text{ g/mol}} \times 100\% = 25.13\%$. Finally, check to see that the total of the calculated percents is 100 %. There may be a slight difference due to rounding. For methane, 74.87% + 25.13 % = 100%.

Balancing Chemical Equations and Stoichiometry

Balancing a chemical equation

According to the law of conservation of mass, the mass of the products must always equal the mass of the reactants in a chemical reaction. Because mass is conserved, the number of each type of atom in the products must equal the number of each type of atom in the reactants. The key to balancing a chemical reaction is in balancing the number of each type of atom on both sides of the equation. Only the coefficients in front of the reactants and products may be changed to accomplish this, not the subscripts in the molecules themselves. Try balancing the largest number of a type of atom first. Also, check if any odd numbers need to be changed to even. Always leave the uncombined elements to balance until the end.

<u>Example #1</u>

Balance the equation $KNO_3 (s) \rightarrow KNO_2 (s) + O_2 (g)$.

First, determine the types and numbers of each type of atom on each side of the equation:

Reactants		Products	
K	1	K	1
N	1	N	1
O	3	O	4

"Oxygen" needs to be balanced. Add a coefficient of "2" to the left side to force "oxygen" to be even and update the counts:

Reactants		Products	
K	2	K	1
N	2	N	1
O	6	O	4

Now, balance the potassium and nitrogen by placing a coefficient of "2" in front of the KNO_2 and update the counts:

Reactants		Products	
K	2	K	2
N	2	N	2
O	6	O	6

The equation is now balanced: $2KNO_3(s) \rightarrow 2KNO_2(s) + O_2(g)$.

Example #2

Balance the equation $C_2H_2(g) + O_2(g) \rightarrow CO_2(g) + H_2O(g)$.

First, determine the types and numbers of each type of atom on each side of the equation:

Reactants		Products	
C	2	C	1
H	2	H	2
O	2	O	3

"Oxygen" needs to be balanced, but remember to leave the uncombined oxygen reactant until the end. "Carbon" also needs to be balanced. Add a coefficient of "4" to the CO_2 on the right side and a coefficient of "2" in front of the C_2H_2 and update the counts:

Reactants		Products	
C	4	C	4
H	4	H	2
O	2	O	9

Balance the "hydrogen" by adding a "2" in front of the H_2O and update the counts:

Reactants		Products	
C	4	C	4
H	4	H	4
O	2	O	10

Finally, balance the "oxygen" by adding a "5" in front of the O_2 on the left.

The equation is now balanced: $2C_2H_2(g) + 5O_2(g) \rightarrow 4CO_2(g) + 2H_2O(g)$.

Balancing a chemical equation involving a simple oxidation-reduction reaction

One method to balance simple oxidation-reduction reactions is to split the reaction into half-reactions. First, write the oxidation half-reaction and the reduction half-reaction.

- 11 -

Remember the phrase *"LEO the lion says GER,"* which is a reminder that the loss of electrons is oxidation, and the gain of electrons is reduction. Next, balance the electrons by multiply the equation(s) by the necessary factor(s). Finally, cancel the electron(s) and combine the balanced oxidation and reduction half-reactions into a balanced net chemical equation.

Example #1

Balance the following chemical equation involving an oxidation-reduction reaction: $Na + O_2 \rightarrow Na^+ + O^{2-}$.

In order to balance the equation $Na + O_2 \rightarrow Na^+ + O^{2-}$, first, write the individual half-reactions:

oxidation: $Na \rightarrow Na^+ + e^-$
reduction: $O_2 + 2e^- \rightarrow O^{2-}$.

Next, balance the number of electrons by multiplying the oxidation half-reaction by 2:

oxidation: $2Na \rightarrow 2Na^+ + 2e^-$
reduction: $O_2 + 2e^- \rightarrow O^{2-}$.

Finally, cancel the electrons and combine the half-reactions into the net reaction:

$2Na + O_2 \rightarrow 2Na^+ + O^{2-}$.

Example #2

Given the following equation at standard temperature and pressure (STP),

$4Fe\ (s) + 3O_2\ (g) \rightarrow 2Fe_2O_3\ (s)$, explain how to determine the volume of $O_2\ (g)$ needed to produce 10.0 moles of $Fe_2O_3\ (s)$.

One method to determine the volume of $O_2\ (g)$ needed to produce 10.0 moles of $Fe_2O_3\ (s)$ is to use dimensional analysis with the mole ratio for the balanced chemical equation. Because 3 moles of $O_2\ (g)$ produce 2 moles of $Fe_2O_3\ (s)$, the needed mole ratio is $\left(\frac{3 \text{ moles } O_2}{2 \text{ moles } Fe_2O_3}\right)$. Also, at STP, one mole of a gas has a volume of 22.4 L. This can be written as a conversion factor of $\left(\frac{22.4 \text{ L}}{1 \text{ mole } O_2}\right)$. Using dimensional analysis, (10.0 mol $Fe_2O_3)\left(\frac{3 \text{ moles } O_2}{2 \text{ moles } Fe_2O_3}\right)\left(\frac{22.4 \text{ L}}{1 \text{ mole } O_2}\right) = 336$ L.

Example #3

Given the following equation at STP,

C_3H_8 (l) + $5O_2$ (g) → $3CO_2$ (g) + $4H_2O$ (g), explain how to determine the volume of O_2 (g) needed to burn 1.00 kg of C_3H_8 (l).

One method to determine the volume of O_2 (g) needed to burn 1.0 kg of C_3H_8 (l) is to use dimensional analysis with conversion factors for the molar mass, number of moles, and liters of gas at STP. The conversion factor for the molar mass of C_3H_8 can be written as $\left(\frac{1 \text{ mol } C_3H_8}{44.1 \text{ grams } C_3H_8}\right)$. Because 1 mole of C_3H_8 (l) requires 5 moles of O_2 (g), the needed mole ratio is $\left(\frac{5 \text{ moles } O_2}{1 \text{ mole } C_3H_8}\right)$. Also, at STP, one mole of a gas has a volume of 22.4 L. This can be written as the conversion factor $\left(\frac{22.4 \text{ L}}{1 \text{ mole } O_2}\right)$. Using dimensional analysis,

$(1.0 \text{ kg of } C_3H_8)\left(\frac{1000 \text{ g}}{1 \text{ kg}}\right)\left(\frac{1 \text{ mole } C_3H_8}{44.1 \text{ g } C_3H_8}\right)\left(\frac{5 \text{ moles } O_2}{1 \text{ mole } C_3H_8}\right)\left(\frac{22.4 \text{ L } O_2}{1 \text{ mole } O_2}\right) = 2.54 \times 10^3 \text{ L}$ O_2.

Example #4

Given the following equation,

2Na (s) + Cl_2 (g) → 2NaCl (s), explain how to determine the amount in grams of Na (s) needed to produce 500.0 g of NaCl (s).

One method to determine the amount in grams of Na (s) needed to produce 500.0 g of NaCl (s) is to use dimensional analysis with conversion factors for the molar mass and number of moles. The conversion factor for the molar mass of NaCl (s) can be written as $\left(\frac{1 \text{ mol NaCl}}{58.44 \text{ g NaCl}}\right)$. Because 2 moles of Na (s) produce 2 moles of NaCl (s), the needed mole ratio is $\left(\frac{2 \text{ moles Na}}{2 \text{ moles NaCl}}\right)$. The conversion factor for the molar mass of Na can be written as $\left(\frac{22.99 \text{ g Na}}{1 \text{ mole Na}}\right)$. Using dimensional analysis, (500.0 g NaCl)$\left(\frac{1 \text{ mol NaCl}}{58.44 \text{ g NaCl}}\right)\left(\frac{2 \text{ moles Na}}{2 \text{ moles NaCl}}\right)\left(\frac{22.99 \text{ g Na}}{1 \text{ mole Na}}\right) = 196.7 \text{ g Na}$.

<u>Example #5</u>

Given the following equation at STP,

2Na (s) + Cl₂ (g) → 2NaCl (s), explain how to determine the volume of Cl_2 (g) needed to produce 1.00 kg of NaCl(s).

One method to determine the volume of Cl_2 (g) needed to produce 1.00 kg of NaCl (s) is to use dimensional analysis with conversion factors for the molar mass, number of moles, and liters of gas at STP. The conversion factor for the molar mass of NaCl can be written as $\left(\frac{1 \text{ mol NaCl}}{58.44 \text{ g NaCl}}\right)$. Because 1 mole of Cl_2 (g) produces 2 moles of NaCl (s), the needed mole ratio is $\left(\frac{1 \text{ mole Cl}_2}{1 \text{ mole NaCl}}\right)$. Also, at STP, one mole of a gas has a volume of 22.4 L. This can be written as a conversion factor $\left(\frac{22.4 \text{ L}}{1 \text{ mole Cl}_2}\right)$. Using dimensional analysis, (1.00 kg NaCl)$\left(\frac{1000 \text{ g}}{1 \text{ kg}}\right)\left(\frac{1 \text{ mol NaCl}}{58.44 \text{ g NaCl}}\right)\left(\frac{1 \text{ mole Cl}_2}{1 \text{ mole NaCl}}\right)\left(\frac{22.4 \text{ L O}_2}{1 \text{ mole O}_2}\right) = 383.299\ldots$ L Cl_2, which rounds up to 384 L because 383 L will not be enough.

Limiting reagent in a reaction

The limiting reagent, or limiting reactant, is the reactant that determines or "limits" the amount of product formed. The limiting reagent is totally consumed in the chemical reaction. The other reactants in the chemical reaction must be present in excess amounts than what is needed. The excess reactants will be left over after the limiting reactant is consumed. To determine the limiting reagent from the balanced chemical equation, select one of the products and calculate how much of that product can be produced from each reactant. The reactant that produces the least amount of that product is the limiting reactant or limiting reagent.

Calculating the percent yield for a chemical reaction

To calculate the percent yield for a chemical reaction, use the formula

$$\text{percent yield} = \frac{\text{actual yield}}{\text{theoretical yield}} \times 100\%.$$

The actual yield should be stated in the problem or determined experimentally. The theoretical yield can be calculated from the balanced chemical equation with dimensional analysis using conversion factors for molar mass and number of moles. Divide the actual yield by the theoretical yield. This is a decimal that can be converted to a percent by multiplying by 100 and adding the percent sign.

<u>Example #1</u>

Given that 100.0 g of H₂ (g) react with 350.0 g of O₂ (g), explain how to determine the limiting reactant and the amount of excess reactant that remains.

$2H_2$ (g) + O_2 (g) → $2H_2O$ (g).

To determine the limiting reactant, first determine the amount of H_2O that can be produced from each of the reactants:

- $(100.0 \text{ g } H_2)\left(\frac{1 \text{ mole } H_2}{2.016 \text{ g } H_2}\right)\left(\frac{2 \text{ moles } H_2O}{2 \text{ moles } H_2}\right)\left(\frac{18.016 \text{ g } H_2O}{1 \text{ mole } H_2O}\right) = 893.7 \text{ g } H_2O.$
- $(350.0 \text{ g } O_2)\left(\frac{1 \text{ mole } O_2}{32.00 \text{ g } O_2}\right)\left(\frac{2 \text{ moles } H_2O}{1 \text{ mole } O_2}\right)\left(\frac{18.016 \text{ g } H_2O}{1 \text{ mole } H_2O}\right) = 394.1 \text{ g } H_2O.$

Because O_2 produces the least amount of H_2O, O_2 is the limiting reagent. Therefore, H_2 is the reactant that is in excess. Calculating the amount of H_2 consumed in this reaction:

- $(350.0 \text{ g } O_2)\left(\frac{1 \text{ mole } O_2}{32.00 \text{ g } O_2}\right)\left(\frac{2 \text{ moles } H_2}{1 \text{ mole } O_2}\right)\left(\frac{2.016 \text{ g } H_2}{1 \text{ mole } H_2}\right) = 44.10 \text{ g } H_2 \text{ (consumed)}.$

Subtracting this amount from the original amount yields the excess amount: 100.0 g H_2 – 44.10 g H_2 = 55.91 g H_2 (excess).

<u>Example #2</u>

Find the percent yield in the following reaction if 200.0 g of solid KClO₃ produced 100.0 g of solid KCl.

$2KClO_3$ (s) → $2KCl$ (s) + $3O_2$ (g).

To calculate the percent yield if 200.0 g of solid $KClO_3$ produced 100.0 g of solid KCl, first calculate the theoretical yield of KCl or the maximum amount of KCl that can be produced:

theoretical yield:
$(200.0 \text{ g } KClO_3)\left(\frac{1 \text{ mole } KClO_3}{122.6 \text{ g } KClO_3}\right)\left(\frac{2 \text{ moles } KCl}{2 \text{ moles } KClO_3}\right)\left(\frac{74.55 \text{ g } KCl}{1 \text{ mole } KCl}\right) = 121.6 \text{ g } KCl.$

The formula to calculate percent yield is percent yield $= \frac{\text{actual yield}}{\text{theoretical yield}} \times$ 100 %. Substituting in the 100.0 g of KCl for the actual yield and the 121.6 g of KCl for the theoretical yield,

percent yield $= \frac{100.0 \text{ g}}{121.6 \text{ g}} \times 100 \% = 82.24 \%.$

<u>Example #3</u>

Balanced equation for the combustion of methane

The molecular formula for methane is CH_4. For a combustion equation, the reactants are methane (CH_4) and oxygen gas (O_2). The products of this combustion reaction are water vapor (H_2O) and carbon dioxide (CO_2). Setting up the equation yields the following reaction:

- $CH_4 (g) + O_2 (g) \rightarrow CO_2 (g) + H_2O (g)$.

This equation must still be balanced. Finally, the combustion of methane is given by the following reaction:

- $CH_4 (g) + 2O_2 (g) \rightarrow CO_2 (g) + 2H_2O (g)$.

<u>Example #4</u>

Balanced equation for the neutralization of hydrochloric acid, KCl (aq), with sodium hydroxide, NaOH (aq)

In a neutralization reaction, an acid reacts with a base to form a salt and water. The salt forms from the cation of the base and the anion of the acid. The salt formed from these reactants is $NaCl$ with the Na^+ from the base and the Cl^- from the acid. Water forms from the remaining H^+ and OH^- ions:

- acid + base $\rightarrow$ salt + water

$HCl (aq) + NaOH (aq) \rightarrow NaCl (aq) + H_2O (l)$.

<u>Example #5</u>

Balanced equation for the decomposition reaction of solid lithium carbonate (Li_2CO_3)

The general form for a decomposition reaction is $AB \rightarrow A + B$. However, this metal oxide has three elements and may at first not seem to fit the general form. When many metal carbonates are heated, they form the metal oxide and carbon dioxide gas. In this case, the products will also be compounds. In this decomposition reaction, when heated, solid lithium oxide decomposes to form solid lithium oxide and gaseous carbon dioxide:

- $Li_2CO_3(s) \xrightarrow{\Delta} LiO(s) + CO_2(g)$.

- 16 -

<u>Example #6</u>
Balanced equation for the dehydration of ethanol

Ethanol (C_2H_5OH) can be dehydrated to produce ethane (C_2H_4). The gaseous ethanol is passed over a hot aluminum oxide catalyst to produce ethane and water.

ethanol $\xrightarrow{\text{aluminum oxide}}$ ethane + water

C_2H_5OH (g) $\xrightarrow{Al_2O_3}$ C_2H_4 (g) + H_2O (l).

This can also be shown in the form of condensed structural formulas:
- $CH_3CH_2OH \xrightarrow{Al_2O_3} CH_2 = CH_2 + H_2O$.

Single- and double-replacement reactions

Single-replacement reactions, which are also known as single-displacement reactions or substitution reactions, have the general form of A + BC → AC + B. An example of a single-replacement reaction is the displacement of hydrogen from hydrochloric acid by zinc metal as given in the following equation:
- Zn (s) + 2HCl (aq) → $ZnCl_2$ (aq) + H_2 (aq)

Double-replacement reactions, which are also known as double-displacement reactions, have the general form of AB + CD → AD + CB. An example of a double-replacement reaction is when aqueous solutions of lead(II) nitrate and potassium iodide react to form solid lead(II) iodide and aqueous potassium nitrate as given by the following equation:
- $Pb(NO_3)_2$ (aq) + 2KI (aq) → PbI_2 (s) + $2KNO_3$ (aq)

<u>Example #7</u>
Identify each reaction type as a single- or double-replacement reaction, and predict the products of the following equations:

1. Mg (s) + 2 H_2O (l) →.
2. $Pb(NO_3)_2$ (aq) + 2 KI (aq) →.

1. This reaction must be a single-replacement reaction because the left side corresponds to the left side of the general equation A + BC → AB + C. In this case, the magnesium replaces some of the hydrogen, and the products are hydrogen gas and magnesium hydroxide.
- Mg (s) + 2H_2O (l) → $Mg(OH)_2$ (aq) + H_2 (g).

2. This reaction must be a double-replacement reaction because the left side corresponds to the left side of the general equation AB + CD → AD + CB. In this case, the Pb^+ cation from the $Pb(NO_3)_2$ bonds with the I^- anion from the KI to form solid PbI_2. The NO_3^- anion from the $Pb(NO_3)_2$ bonds with the K^+ cation from the KI to form aqueous KNO_3. $Pb(NO_3)_2$ (aq) + 2KI (aq) → PbI_2 (s) + $2KNO_3$ (aq).

Example #8

Balanced equation for the oxidation-reduction reaction of metallic zinc powder and aqueous copper(II) sulfate

According to the activity series, zinc is more reactive than copper. Therefore, the zinc is oxidized, and the copper is reduced. Write the half-reactions:

- oxidation: $Zn \rightarrow Zn^{2+} + 2e^-$.
- reduction: $Cu^{2+} + 2e^- \rightarrow Cu$.

Cancel the electrons and combine the two half-reactions into the net equation:

- $Zn + Cu^{2+} \rightarrow Zn^{2+} + Cu$.

Finally, add the symbols to indicate the state of each reactant and product:

- $Zn\ (s) + Cu^{2+}\ (aq) \rightarrow Zn^{2+}\ (aq) + Cu\ (s)$.

Interestingly, this equation can also be written as the following single-displacement reaction:

- $Zn\ (s) + CuSO_4\ (aq) \rightarrow ZnSO_4\ (aq) + Cu\ (s)$.

This single-displacement reaction has the same net ionic equation after canceling out the spectator ions.

Example #9

Balanced equation for the oxidation-reduction reaction of a piece of solid copper wire immersed in an aqueous solution of silver nitrate

According to the activity series, copper is more reactive than silver. Therefore, the copper is oxidized, and the silver is reduced. Write the half-reactions:

- oxidation: $Cu \rightarrow Cu^{2+} + 2e^-$.
- reduction: $Ag^+ + e^- \rightarrow Ag$.

Multiply the reduction half-reaction by 2 to balance the number of electrons:

- oxidation: $Cu \rightarrow Cu^{2+} + 2e^-$.
- reduction: $2Ag^+ + 2e^- \rightarrow 2Ag$.

Cancel the electrons and combine the two half-reactions into the net equation:

- $Cu + 2Ag^+ \rightarrow Cu^{2+} + 2Ag$.

Finally, add the symbols to indicate the state of each reactant and product:

- $Cu\ (s) + 2Ag^+\ (aq) \rightarrow Cu^{2+}\ (aq) + 2Ag\ (s)$.

Note that this equation is also classified as a single-displacement reaction:

- $Cu\ (s) + 2AgNO_3\ (aq) \rightarrow Cu(NO_3)_2\ (aq) + 2Ag\ (s)$.

This single-displacement reaction has the same net ionic equation after canceling out the spectator ions.

Solutions and Solubility

Dilute and concentrated

The terms *dilute* and *concentrated* have opposite meanings. In a solution, the solute is dissolved in the solvent. The more solute that is dissolved, the more concentrated is the solution. The less solute that is dissolved, the less concentrated and the more dilute is the solution. The terms are often associated with the preparation of a stock solution for a laboratory experiment. Stock solutions are typically ordered in a concentrated solution. To prepare for use in a chemistry lab, the stock solutions are diluted to the appropriate molarity by adding a specific amount of solvent such as water to a specific amount of stock solution.

Saturated, unsaturated, and supersaturated

The terms *saturated, unsaturated,* and *supersaturated* are associated with solutions. In a solution, a solute is added to a solvent. In a saturated solution, the solute is added to the solvent until no more solute is able to dissolve. The undissolved solute will settle down to the bottom of the beaker. A solution is considered unsaturated as long as more solute is able to go into solution under ordinary conditions. The solubility of solids in liquids typically increases as temperature increases. If the temperature of a solution is increased as the solute is being added, more solute than is normally possible may go into solution, forming a supersaturated solution.

Solvent and solute

A solution is a homogeneous mixture that consists of a solute and a solvent. In general terms, the solute is the substance that is being dissolved and the solvent is the substance doing the dissolving. Ionic compounds dissociate, and molecular compounds ionize in solution. Typically, the solute is the substance that is present in the greater amount and the solvent is the substance that is present in the lesser amount. For example, in a glucose solution, the glucose would be considered the solute, and the water would be considered the solvent.

Calculating the molarity and molality of a solution

Molarity and molality are measures of the concentration of a solution. Molarity (M) is the amount of solute in moles per the amount of solution in liters. A 1.0 M solution consists of 1.0 mole of solute for each 1.0 L of solution. Molality (m) is the amount of solute in moles per the amount of solvent in kilograms. A 1.0 m solution consists of 1.0 mole of solute for each 1.0 kg of solvent. Often, when performing these calculations, the amount of solute is given in grams. To convert from grams of solute to moles of solute, multiply the grams of solute by the molar mass of the solute:

- Molarity (M) = $\frac{\text{moles of solute (mol)}}{\text{liters of solution (L)}}$. Molality (m) = $\frac{\text{moles of solute (mol)}}{\text{kilograms of solvent (kg)}}$.

Calculating mole fraction, parts per million, parts per billion, and percent by mass or volume

Concentrations can be measured in mole fractions, parts per million, parts per billion, and percent by mass or volume. Mole fraction (χ) is calculated by dividing the number of moles of one component by the total number of moles of all of the components of the solution. Parts per million (ppm) is calculated by dividing the mass of the solute in grams by the mass of the solvent and solute in grams and then multiplying the quotient by 1,000,000 ppm. Parts per billion (ppb) is calculated similarly, except the quotient is multiplied by 1,000,000,000 ppb. Percent concentration can be calculated by mass or by volume by dividing the mass or volume of the solute by the mass or volume of the solution. This quotient is a decimal that can be converted to a percent by multiplying by 100.

Calculating the molarity of 100.0 g of CaCl₂ in 500.0 mL of solution

To calculate molarity, use the formula molarity (M) = $\frac{\text{moles of solute (mol)}}{\text{liters of solution (L)}}$. The necessary conversions from grams $CaCl_2$ to moles $CaCl_2$ and from 500.0 mL to liters may be performed using dimensional analysis. An alternate method of working this problem would be doing the conversions first and then substituting those values directly into the equation. Using the method of dimensional analysis and substituting the given information into the equation yields molarity = $\frac{100.0 \text{ grams } CaCl_2}{500.0 \text{ mL of solution}}$. Adding the necessary conversions using dimensional analysis yields

$$\text{molarity} = \left(\frac{100.0 \text{ g } CaCl_2}{500.0 \text{ mL of solution}}\right)\left(\frac{\text{mol } CaCl_2}{110.98 \text{ g}}\right)\left(\frac{1000 \text{ mL}}{L}\right) = 1.802 \text{ M}.$$

Preparing a dilute solution from a stock solution

In order to prepare a dilute solution from a stock solution, the molarity and the needed volume of the diluted solution as well as the molarity of the stock solution must be known. The volume of the stock solution to be diluted can be calculated using the formula $V_{stock}M_{stock}$ = $V_{dilute}M_{dilute}$, where V_{stock} is the unknown variable, M_{stock} is the molarity of the stock solution, V_{dilute} is the needed volume of the dilute solution, and M_{dilute} is the needed molarity of the dilute solution. Solving this formula for V_{stock} yields $V_{stock} = \frac{V_{dilute}M_{dilute}}{M_{stock}}$. Then, dilute the calculated amount of stock solution (V_{stock}) to the total volume required of the diluted solution.

Effects of temperature, pressure, surface area, and agitation on the dissolution rate

Temperature, pressure, surface area, and agitation affect the dissolution rate. Increasing the temperature increases the kinetic energy of the molecules, which increases the number of collisions with the solute particles. Increasing the surface area of contact by stirring (agitation) or crushing a solid solute also increases the dissolution rate and helps prevent recrystallization. Increasing the pressure will increase the dissolution rate for gas solutes in liquid solvents because the added pressure will make it more difficult for the gas to escape.

Increasing the pressure will have virtually no effect on the dissolution rate for solid solutes in liquid solvents under normal conditions.

Effect of temperature and pressure on solubility

Temperature and pressure affect solubility. For gas solutes in liquid solvents, increasing the temperature increases the kinetic energy causing more gas particles to escape the surface of the liquid solvents and therefore decreasing the solubility of the solutes. For most solid solutes in liquid solvents, increasing the temperature increases the solubility, as shown in this solubility curve for selected salts. For gas solutes in liquid solvents, increasing the pressure increases the solubility. Increasing the pressure of liquid or solid solutes in liquid solvents has virtually no effect under normal conditions.

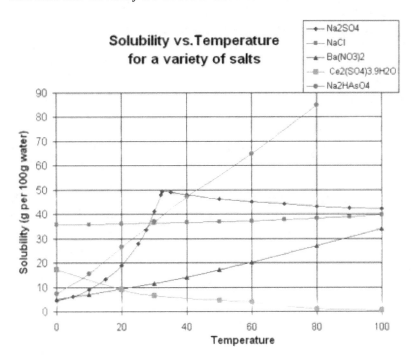

Freezing point depression

Freezing point depression is a colligative property of solutions that depends only on the number of particles in solution, not on the identity of those particles. Adding a nonvolatile solute to a solution will lower the freezing point of that solution. This decrease in temperature is known as *freezing point depression*. Basically, the particles of the nonvolatile solute occupy spaces near the surface and block or inhibit the solvent particles from escaping from the surface of the solution. As fewer particles escape, the vapor pressure lowers. This decrease in vapor pressure causes a decrease in the freezing point known as freezing point depression. The amount of depression can be calculated from the equation $\Delta T_{FP} = mk_f$, where m is the molality of the solution and k_f is the molal freezing point constant for that particular solvent.

Boiling point elevation

Boiling point elevation is a colligative property of solutions that depends only on the number of particles in solution, not on the identity of those particles. Adding a nonvolatile

- 21 -

solute to a solution will raise the boiling point of that solution. This rise in temperature is known as boiling point elevation. Basically, the particles of the nonvolatile solute occupy spaces near the surface and block or inhibit the solvent particles from escaping from the surface of the solution. As fewer particles escape, the vapor pressure lowers. This decrease in vapor pressure causes an increase in the boiling point known as *boiling point elevation*. The amount of elevation can be calculated from the equation $\Delta T_{BP} = mk_b$, where m is the molality of the solution and k_b is the molal boiling point constant for that particular solvent.

Vapor pressure lowering

Vapor pressure lowering is a colligative property of solutions that depends only on the number of particles in solution, not on the identity of those particles. Adding a nonvolatile solute to a solution will lower the vapor pressure of that solution. Basically, the particles of the nonvolatile solute occupy spaces near the surface and block or inhibit the solvent particles from escaping from the surface of the solution. As fewer particles escape, the vapor pressure lowers. This decrease in vapor pressure causes an increase in the boiling point and a decrease in the freezing point.

Osmosis

Osmosis can be defined as diffusion through a semipermeable membrane. Typically, small solvent particles can pass through, but larger solute particles are too large to pass through. This means that osmosis is the net flow of solvent from a solution with a lower concentration to a solution with a higher concentration until a state of equilibrium is reached. The pressure that must be applied to the semipermeable membrane to stop the flow of solvent to reach this equilibrium state is called *osmotic pressure*. Osmotic pressure is a colligative property that depends on the number of nonvolatile solute particles, not the identity.

Atomic Structure

Organization of Matter

Pure substances

Pure substances are substances that cannot be further broken down into simpler substances and still retain their characteristics. Pure substances are categorized as either elements or compounds. Elements that consist of only one type of atom may be monatomic, diatomic, or polyatomic. For example, helium (He) and copper (Cu) are monatomic elements, and hydrogen (H_2) and oxygen (O_2) are diatomic elements. Phosphorus (P_4) and sulfur (S_8) are polyatomic elements. Compounds consist of molecules of more than one type of atom. For example, pure water (H_2O) is made up of molecules consisting of two atoms of hydrogen bonded to one atom of oxygen, and glucose ($C_6H_{12}O_6$) is made up of molecules of six carbon atoms and twelve hydrogen atoms bonded together with six oxygen atoms.

Mixtures

Mixtures can be classified as either homogeneous mixtures or heterogeneous mixtures. The molecules of homogeneous mixtures are distributed uniformly throughout the mixture, but the molecules of heterogeneous mixtures are not distributed uniformly throughout the mixture. Air is an example of a homogeneous mixture, and a pile of sand and salt is an example of a heterogeneous mixture. Solutions are homogeneous mixtures consisting of a solute, the substance that is dissolved, and a solvent, the substance doing the dissolving. Examples of solutions include vinegar (a solution of acetic acid in water) and sugar dissolved in water. Suspensions are heterogeneous mixtures in which the particle size of the substance suspended is too large to be kept in suspension by Brownian motion. Once left undisturbed, suspensions will settle out to form layers. An example of a suspension is sand stirred into water. Left undisturbed, the sand will fall out of suspension and the water will form a layer on top of the sand.

Matter

The four states of matter are solids, liquids, gases, and plasma. Solids have a definite shape and a definite volume. Because solid particles are held in fairly rigid positions, solids are the least compressible of the four states of matter. Liquids have definite volumes but no definite shapes. Because their particles are free to slip and slide over each other, liquids take the shape of their containers, but they still remain fairly incompressible by natural means. Gases have no definite shape or volume. Because gas particles are free to move, they move away from each other causing gases to fill their containers. This also makes gases very compressible. Plasmas are high-temperature, ionized gases that exist only under very high temperatures at which electrons are stripped away from their atoms.

Particulate Structure of Matter

Atoms and ions

Neutral atoms have equal numbers of protons and electrons. Some atoms tend to lose electrons in order to have a full outer shell of valence electrons and become positively charged ions or cations. For example, the alkali metals sodium and potassium form the cations Na^+ and K^+, and the alkaline earth metals magnesium and calcium form the cations Mg^{2+} and Ca^{2+}. Some atoms tend to gain electrons to fill their outer shells and become negatively charged ions or anions. For example, the halogens fluorine and chlorine form the anions F^- and Cl^-, and the chalcogens oxygen and sulfur form the anions O^{2-} and S^{2-}

Atoms and molecules

Atoms are the smallest particles of an element that still retain the properties of that element. For example, a copper atom is the smallest piece of a copper wire that still has the properties of copper. Molecules are made of two or more atoms. Molecules are the smallest particles of a compound that still retain the properties of that compound. For example, the substance water consists of water molecules of two hydrogen atoms covalently bonded to one oxygen atom. A water molecule is the smallest particle of water that still has the properties of water. Also, elements may be diatomic or polyatomic molecules. For example, hydrogen gas (H_2) exists naturally as diatomic molecules. In this case, the molecule could be further broken down into individual hydrogen atoms.

Chemical/Physical Properties/Changes

Chemical and physical properties

Matter has both physical and chemical properties. Physical properties can be seen or observed without changing the identity or composition of matter. For example, the mass, volume, and density of a substance can be determined without permanently changing the sample. Other physical properties include color, boiling point, freezing point, solubility, odor, hardness, electrical conductivity, thermal conductivity, ductility, and malleability. Chemical properties cannot be measured without changing the identity or composition of matter. Chemical properties describe how a substance reacts or changes to form a new substance. Examples of chemical properties include flammability, corrosivity, oxidation states, enthalpy of formation, and reactivity with other chemicals.

Chemical and physical changes

Physical changes do not produce new substances. The atoms or molecules may be rearranged, but no new substances are formed. Phase changes or changes of state such as melting, freezing, and sublimation are physical changes. For example, physical changes include the melting of ice, the boiling of water, sugar dissolving into water, and the crushing of a piece of chalk into a fine powder. Chemical changes involve a chemical reaction and do produce new substances. When iron rusts, iron oxide is formed, indicating a chemical change. Other examples of chemical changes include baking a cake, burning wood, digesting a cracker, and mixing an acid and a base.

Intensive and extensive properties

Physical properties are categorized as either intensive or extensive. Intensive properties *do not* depend on the amount of matter or quantity of the sample. This means that intensive properties will not change if the sample size is increased or decreased. Intensive properties include color, hardness, melting point, boiling point, density, ductility, malleability, specific heat, temperature, concentration, and magnetization. Extensive properties *do* depend on the amount of matter or quantity of the sample. Therefore, extensive properties do change if the sample size is increased or decreased. If the sample size is increased, the property increases. If the sample size is decreased, the property decreases. Extensive properties include volume, mass, weight, energy, entropy, number of moles, and electrical charge.

Current Model of Atomic Structure / Electron Configuration

Subatomic particles

The three major subatomic particles are the proton, neutron, and electron. The proton, which is located in the nucleus, has a relative charge of +1. The neutron, which is located in the nucleus, has a relative charge of 0. The electron, which is located outside the nucleus, has a relative charge of –1. The proton and neutron, which are essentially the same mass, are much more massive than the electron and make up the mass of the atom. The electron's mass is insignificant compared to the mass of the proton and neutron.

Orbits and orbitals

An orbit is a definite path, but an orbital is a region in space. The Bohr model described electrons as orbiting or following a definite path in space around the nucleus of an atom. But, according to the uncertainty principle, it is impossible to determine the location and the momentum of an electron simultaneously. Therefore, it is impossible to draw a definite path or orbit of an electron. An orbital as described by the quantum-mechanical model or the electron-cloud model is a region in space that is drawn in such a way as to indicate the probability of finding an electron at a specific location. The distance an orbital is located from the nucleus corresponds to the principal quantum number. The orbital shape corresponds to the subshell or azimuthal quantum number. The orbital orientation corresponds to the magnetic quantum number.

Quantum numbers

The principal quantum number (n) describes an electron's shell or energy level and actually describes the size of the orbital. Electrons farther from the nucleus are at higher energy levels. The subshell or azimuthal quantum number (l) describes the electron's sublevel or subshell (s, *p, d,* or *f*) and specifies the shape of the orbital. Typical shapes include spherical, dumbbell, and clover leaf. The magnetic quantum number (m_l) describes the orientation of the orbital in space. The spin or magnetic moment quantum number (m_s) describes the direction of the spin of the electron in the orbital.

Atomic number and mass number

The atomic number of an element is the number of protons in the nucleus of an atom of that element. This is the number that identifies the type of an atom. For example, all oxygen atoms have eight protons, and all carbon atoms have six protons. Each element is identified by its specific atomic number. The mass number is the number of protons and neutrons in the nucleus of an atom. Although the atomic number is the same for all atoms of a specific element, the mass number can vary due to the varying numbers of neutrons in various isotopes of the atom.

Isotope

Isotopes are atoms of the same element that vary in their number of neutrons. Isotopes of the same element have the same number of protons and thus the same atomic number. But, because isotopes vary in the number of neutrons, they can be identified by their mass numbers. For example, two naturally occurring carbon isotopes are carbon-12 and carbon-13, which have mass numbers 12 and 13, respectively. The symbols $^{12}_{6}C$ and $^{13}_{6}C$ also represent the carbon isotopes. The general form of the symbol is $^{M}_{A}X$, where X represents the element symbol, M represents the mass number, and A represents the atomic number.

Average atomic mass

The average atomic mass is the weighted average of the masses of all the naturally occurring isotopes of an atom. The unit for average atomic mass is the atomic mass unit (u), which is defined as 1/12 the mass of a single atom of carbon-12. Atomic masses of isotopes are measured using a mass spectrometer by bombarding a gaseous sample of the isotope and measuring its relative deflections. Atomic masses can be calculated if the percent abundances and the atomic masses of the naturally occurring isotopes are known.

Aufbau principle

The *Aufbau principle* is named from the German word for "building up," and it describes how electrons fill the energy levels or shells of an atom. In general, electrons will fill the $n = 1$ energy level before filling the $n = 2$ energy level, and electrons will fill the $n = 2$ energy level before filling the $n = 3$ energy level. The s subshell of an energy level will fill before the p subshell, which fills before the d and f subshells.

Hund's rule

Hund's rule describes how electrons fill the orbitals in a sublevel. Less energy is required for an electron to occupy an orbital alone than the energy needed for an electron to pair up with another electron in an orbital. Therefore, electrons will occupy each orbital in a subshell before electrons will begin to pair up in those orbitals. For example, in the $2p$ subshell, one electron will occupy each of the three orbitals before pairing begins. In the $3d$ subshell, one electron will occupy each of the five orbitals before pairing begins.

Pauli exclusion principle

The *Pauli exclusion principle* describes the unique address or location of each electron in an atom. Each electron has a unique or exclusive set of four quantum numbers indicating the electron's energy level, subshell, orbital orientation, and magnetic moment. Every orbital can hold a maximum of two electrons, but even if two electrons occupy the same orbital resulting in identical energy levels, subshells, and orbital orientations, they must have opposite spins, which means that their magnetic moment quantum numbers will differ.

Electron configuration and the periodic table

Electron configurations show a direct correlation to the periodic table. The periodic table can be divided into blocks representing *s, p, d,* and *f* subshells. The energy level corresponds to the row or period of the periodic table. The subshells, *s, p, d,* or *f* are related to the block's group numbers. The *s* block corresponds to groups 1A and 2A. The *p* block corresponds to groups 3A–8A.

The *d* block corresponds to the 10 groups of transition metals, and the *f* block corresponds to the two rows of inner transition metals (14 groups) located at the bottom of the table.

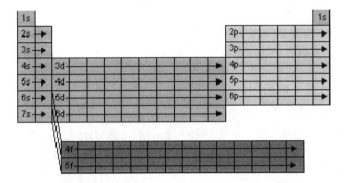

Electron configuration and chemical and physical properties

The chemical and physical properties of atoms are related to the number of valence electrons the atom possesses. Atoms (except hydrogen and helium) seek to have eight electrons in their outer shell as stated in the octet rule. A full octet corresponds to full *s* and *p* orbitals. Noble gases all have full *s* and *p* orbitals and are inert. To fulfill the octet rule, elements in groups 1A (alkali metals) and 2A (alkaline earth metals) tend to lose one or two electrons, respectively, forming cations. Elements in group 6A (chalcogens) and group 7A (halogens) tend to gain one or two electrons, respectively, forming anions. Other elements such as carbon (group 4A) tend to form covalent bonds to satisfy the octet rule.

Cathode ray tube (CRT)

Electrons were discovered by Joseph John Thomson through scientific work with CRTs. Cathode rays had been studied for many years, but it was Thomson who showed that cathode rays were negatively charged particles. Although Thomson could not determine an electron's charge or mass, he was able to determine the ratio of the charge to the mass. Thomson discovered that this ratio was constant regardless of the gas in the CRT. He was able to show that the cathode rays were actually streams of negatively charged particles by deflecting them with a positively charged plate.

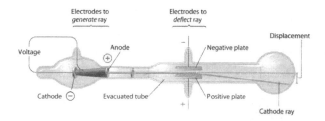

Gold foil experiment

After Thomson determined the ratio of the charge to the mass of an electron from studying cathode rays, he proposed the plum pudding model, in which he compared electrons to the raisins embedded in plum pudding. This model of the atom was disproved by the gold foil experiment. The gold foil experiment led to the discovery of the nucleus of an atom. Scientists at Rutherford's laboratory bombarded a thin gold foil with high-speed helium ions. Much to their surprise, some of the ions were reflected by the foil. The scientists concluded that the atom has a hard central core, which we now know to be the nucleus.

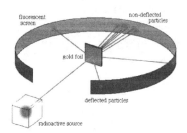

Problems that Rutherford's model had with spectral lines and how the Bohr model solved those problems

Rutherford's model allowed for the electrons of an atom to be in an infinite number of orbits based on Newton's laws of motion. Rutherford believed that electrons could orbit the nucleus at any distance from the nucleus and that electrons could change velocity and direction at any moment. But, according to Rutherford's model, the electrons would lose energy and spiral into the nucleus. Unfortunately, if this was in fact true, then every atom would be unstable. Rutherford's model also does not correspond to the spectral lines emitted from gases at low pressure. The spectral lines are discrete bands of light at specific energy levels. These spectral lines indicate that electrons must be at specific distances from the nucleus. If electrons could be located at any distance from the nucleus, then these gases should emit continuous spectra instead of spectral lines.

Electronic Absorption and Emission Spectra

Electronic energy transition (emission/absorption of energy) in atoms

An electron must gain or absorb energy to transition to a higher or excited state, and the electron will emit that energy when it transitions back to the ground state. The ground state of an electron is the electron's lowest state of energy or when the electron is in the energy level that it normally occupies. An electron can gain energy if it absorbs a photon or collides with another particle. When an electron occupies an energy level higher that its normal level or ground state, it is in an excited state. The excited state is an unstable state, and the electron will return to the ground state as quickly as possible.

Electronic absorption/emission spectral lines

The emission spectrum of a substance is a specific pattern of bright lines, bands, or continuous radiation that is determined by the frequencies of the electromagnetic spectrum that are emitted due to an electron's transition from a higher state to a lower state. The absorption spectrum is the electromagnetic spectrum interrupted by a specific pattern of dark bands that is determined by the frequencies of the electromagnetic spectrum that are absorbed by a particular substance. The number of lines in the emission spectrum equals the number of lines in the absorption spectrum for a particular substance. In the emission spectrum and the absorption spectrum, the frequencies correspond to the orbitals of the atoms that are involved. A substance can be identified by its emission spectrum or its absorption spectrum.

Energy, frequency, and wavelength

The properties of energy, frequency, and wavelength can be used to describe electromagnetic waves. These properties also have a mathematic relationship between each other. Energy (E) is directly related to frequency (f) as given by $E = hf$, where h represents Planck's constant (6.626×10^{-34} J·s). As the frequency increases, the energy increases. For example, gamma rays, which have the highest frequency of the electromagnetic spectrum, also have the highest energy. The speed (v) of the wave is equal to the product of the wavelength (λ) and frequency (f). Because the speed of light (c) is constant in a vacuum at 3.00×10^8 m/s, the wavelength and frequency are inversely related. As the wavelength decreases, frequency increases. For example, gamma rays have the shortest wavelength of the electromagnetic spectrum and the highest frequency.

Periodicity

Groups and periods in the periodic table

A group is a vertical column of the periodic table. Elements in the same group have the same number of valence electrons. For the representative elements, the number of valence electrons is equal to the group number. Because of their equal valence electrons, elements in the same groups have similar physical and chemical properties. A period is a horizontal row of the periodic table. Atomic number increases from left to right across a row. The period of an element corresponds to the highest energy level of the electrons in the atoms of that element. The energy level increases from top to bottom down a group.

Atomic number and atomic mass in the periodic table

The elements in the periodic table are arranged in order of increasing atomic number first left to right and then top to bottom across the periodic table. The atomic number represents the number of protons in the atoms of that element. Because of the increasing numbers of protons, the atomic mass typically also increases from left to right across a period and from top to bottom down a row. The atomic mass is a weighted average of all the naturally occurring isotopes of an element.

Assigning atomic symbols to elements

The atomic symbol for many elements is simply the first letter of the element name. For example, the atomic symbol for hydrogen is H, and the atomic symbol for carbon is C. The atomic symbol of other elements is the first two letters of the element name. For example, the atomic symbol for helium is He, and the atomic symbol for cobalt is Co. The atomic symbols of several elements are derived from Latin. For example, the atomic symbol for copper (Cu) is derived from *cuprum,* and the atomic symbol for iron (Fe) is derived from *ferrum.* The atomic symbol for tungsten (W) is derived from the German word *wolfram.*

Arrangement of metals, nonmetals, and metalloids in the periodic table

The metals are located on the left side and center of the periodic table, and the nonmetals are located on the right side of the periodic table. The metalloids or semimetals form a zigzag line between the metals and nonmetals as shown below. Metals include the alkali metals such as lithium, sodium, and potassium and the alkaline earth metals such as beryllium, magnesium, and calcium. Metals also include the transition metals such as iron, copper, and nickel and the inner transition metals such as thorium, uranium, and plutonium. Nonmetals include the chalcogens such as oxygen and sulfur, the halogens such as fluorine and chlorine, and the noble gases such as helium and argon. Carbon, nitrogen, and phosphorus are also nonmetals.

Metalloids or semimetals include boron, silicon, germanium, antimony, and polonium.

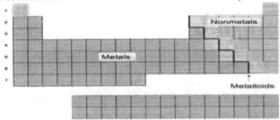

Arrangement of the transition elements

The transition elements belong to one of two categories consisting of the transition metals and the inner transition metals. The transition metals are located in the middle of the periodic table, and the inner transition metals are typically set off as two rows by themselves at the bottom of the periodic table. The transition metals correspond to the "*d* block" for orbital filling, and the inner transition metals correspond to the "*f* block" for orbital filling. Examples of transition metals include iron, copper, nickel, and zinc. The inner transition metals consist of the *lanthanide* or *rare-earth series*, which corresponds to the first row, and the *actinide series*, which corresponds to the second row of the inner transition metals. The *lanthanide series* includes lanthanum, cerium, and praseodymium. The *actinide series* includes actinium, uranium, and plutonium.

Atomic radius size

Atomic radius size decreases across a period from left to right and increases down a group from top to bottom. The atomic radius decreases across a period due to the increasing number of protons and the attraction between those protons and the orbiting electrons. The atomic radius increases down a group due to the increasing energy levels. Atoms in the top-right corner of the periodic table (including hydrogen) have the smallest atomic radii, and atoms in the bottom-left corner of the periodic table have the largest atomic radii. Helium has the smallest atomic radius, and cesium has the largest confirmed atomic radius.

Ionic radius size

The ionic radius size increases down a group of the periodic table. This is due to the increasing energy levels and the fact that electrons are orbiting farther and farther from the nucleus. The trend seen across the periods of the periodic table is due to the formation of cations or anions. Metals form cations or positive ions. Cations are smaller than their neutral atoms due to the loss of one or more electrons. Nonmetals except the noble gases form anions or negative ions. Anions are larger than their neutral atoms due to the gain of one or more electrons.

Ionization energy

Ionization energy is the amount of energy needed to remove an electron from an isolated atom. Ionization energy decreases down a group of the periodic table because the electrons get farther and farther from the nucleus making it easier for the electron to be removed. Ionization energy increases across a period of the periodic table due to the decreasing atomic size, which is due to the increasing number of protons attracting the electrons towards the nucleus. These trends of ionization energy are the opposite of the trends for atomic radius.

Electron affinity

Electron affinity is the energy required to add an electron to a neutral atom in the gaseous phase of an element. Electron affinity values typically range from less negative to more negative. If electrons are added to a halogen such as fluorine or chlorine, energy is released and the electron affinity is negative. If electrons are added to an alkaline earth metal, energy is absorbed and the electron affinity is positive. In general, electron affinity becomes more negative from left to right across a period in the periodic table. Electron affinity becomes less negative from the top to the bottom of a group of the periodic table.

Electronegativity

Electronegativity is a measure of the ability of an atom that is chemically combined to at least one other atom in a molecule to attract electrons to it. The Pauling scale is commonly used to assign values to the elements, with fluorine, which is the most electronegative element, being assigned a value of 4.0. Electronegativity increases from left to right across a period of the periodic table and decreases from top to bottom down a group of the periodic table.

Physical properties of the elements including boiling/melting points and conductivity

The boiling point, melting point, and conductivity of the elements depend partially on the number of valence electrons of the atoms of those elements. For the representative elements in groups 1A–8A, the number of valence electrons matches the group number. Because all of the elements in each individual group contain the same number of valence electrons, elements in the same groups tend to have similar boiling points, melting points, and conductivity. Boiling points and melting points tend to decrease moving down the column of groups 1A–4A and 8A but increase slightly moving down the column of groups 5A–7A.

Chemical reactivity

Atoms of elements in the same group or family of the periodic table tend to have similar chemical properties and similar chemical reactions. For example, the alkali metals, which form cations with a charge of 1+, tend to react with water to form hydrogen gas and metal hydroxides. The alkaline earth metals, which form cations with a charge of 2+, react with oxygen gas to form metal oxides. The halogens, which form anions with a charge of 1–, are highly reactive and toxic. The noble gases are unreactive and never form compounds naturally.

Chemical Bonding and Structure

Bond types

Chemical bonds are the attractive forces that bind atoms together into molecules. Atoms form chemical bonds in an attempt to satisfy the octet rule. These bond types include covalent bonds, ionic bonds, and metallic bonds. Covalent bonds are formed from the sharing of electron pairs between two atoms in a molecule. Ionic bonds are formed from the transferring of electrons between one atom and another, which results in the formations of cations and anions. Metallic bonding results from the sharing of delocalized electrons among all of the atoms in a molecule.

Ionic bonding

Ionic bonding results from the transfer of electrons between atoms. A cation or positive ion is formed when an atom loses one or more electrons. An anion or negative ion is formed when an atom gains one or more electrons. An ionic bond results from the electrostatic attraction between a cation and an anion. One example of a compound formed by ionic bonds is sodium chloride or NaCl. Sodium (Na) is an alkali metal and tends to form Na⁺ ions. Chlorine is a halogen and tends to form Cl⁻ ions. The Na⁺ ion and the Cl⁻ ion are attracted to each other. This electrostatic attraction between these oppositely charged ions is what results in the ionic bond between them.

$$Na \cdot + \overset{\times \ \times}{\underset{\times \ \times}{\times Cl \times}} \longrightarrow [Na]^+ [\overset{\times \ \times}{\underset{\times \ \times}{\colon Cl \times}}]^-$$

electron transer from
sodium to chlorine

Covalent bonding

Covalent bonding results from the sharing of electrons between atoms. Atoms seek to fill their valence shell and will share electrons with another atom in order to have a full octet (except hydrogen and helium, which only hold two electrons in their valence shells). Molecular compounds have covalent bonds. Organic compounds such as proteins, carbohydrates, lipids, and nucleic acids are molecular compounds formed by covalent bonds. Methane (CH_4) is a molecular compound in which one carbon atom is covalently bonded to four hydrogen atoms as shown below.

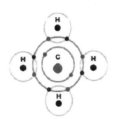

- 33 -

Polar covalent bonds, nonpolar covalent bonds, and hybridization

Polar covalent bonds result when electrons are shared unequally between atoms. Nonpolar covalent bonds result when electrons are shared equally between atoms. The unequal sharing of electrons is due to the differences in the electronegativities of the two atoms sharing the electrons. Partial charges develop due to this unequal sharing of electrons. The greater that the difference is in the electronegativities between the two atoms, the stronger the dipole is. For example, the covalent bonds formed between the carbon atom and the two oxygen atoms in carbon dioxide are polar covalent bonds because the electronegativities of carbon and oxygen differ slightly. If the electronegativities are equal, then the covalent bonds are nonpolar. For example, the covalent double bond between two oxygen atoms is nonpolar because the oxygen atoms have the same electronegativities.

Relative bond lengths of covalent bonds

The bond length of a covalent bond is the distance between the nuclei of two covalently bonded atoms. The higher the bond order, the shorter the bond length. Single bonds are between one pair of electrons, and they are the weakest. Because single bonds (bond order 1) are the weakest, they are the longest of the three types of covalent bonds. Double bonds are between two pairs of electrons. Because double bonds (bond order 2) are stronger that single bonds, double bonds are shorter than single bonds. Triple bonds are between three pairs of electrons. Because triple bonds (bond order 3) are stronger than double bonds and single bonds, triple bonds have the shortest bond length.

Relative bond strengths of covalent bonds

The bond strength determines the amount of energy needed to break a covalent bond. Bond strength increases as bond length decreases. The bond length is the distance between the nuclei of two covalently bonded atoms. The higher the bond order, the shorter the bond length. Single bonds are between one pair of electrons, and they are the weakest. Double bonds are between two pairs of electrons. Double bonds (bond order 2) are stronger that single bonds. Triple bonds are between three pairs of electrons. Triple bonds (bond order 3) are stronger than double bonds and single bonds.

Metallic bonding

Metallic bonding is a type of bonding between metals. Metallic bonds are similar to covalent bonds in that they are a type of sharing of electrons between atoms. However, in covalent bonding, the electrons are shared with only one other atom. In metallic bonding, the electrons are shared with all the surrounding atoms. These electrons are referred to as delocalized electrons. Metallic bonding is responsible for many of the characteristics in metals including conductivity of heat and electricity, malleability, and ductility. An example of metallic bonding is the metallic bond between the copper atoms in a piece of copper wire.

Lewis structure

In order to draw a Lewis structure for a molecule, determine the number of valence electrons for each atom in the molecule and the number of valence electrons each atom needs in order to have a full outer shell. All atoms except hydrogen and helium seek to have eight electrons in their outer shells. Hydrogen and helium only have room for two valence electrons. Next, determine the central atom. Usually, the central atom is the atom with the largest number of valence openings. Draw the skeletal structure with the central atom. Each single bond represents two electrons. Each double bond represents four electrons. Each triple bond represents six electrons. Start with single bonds and change to double or triple bonds as needed to satisfy the octet rule. But remember, atoms may only share what they have available. For example, elements in group IIIA have three valence electrons and need an additional five electrons to make eight, but they may only share the three that they have available. Add the remaining valence electrons to all the atoms. Check to make sure that each atom (except hydrogen, helium, and boron) satisfies the octet rule.

Example Lewis structures

NH_3

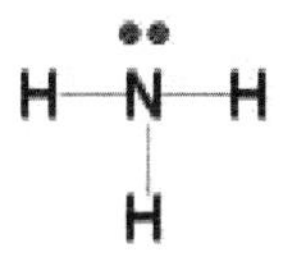

H_2O

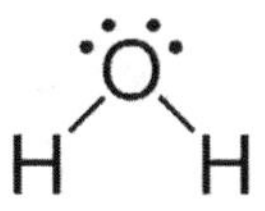

CCl_4

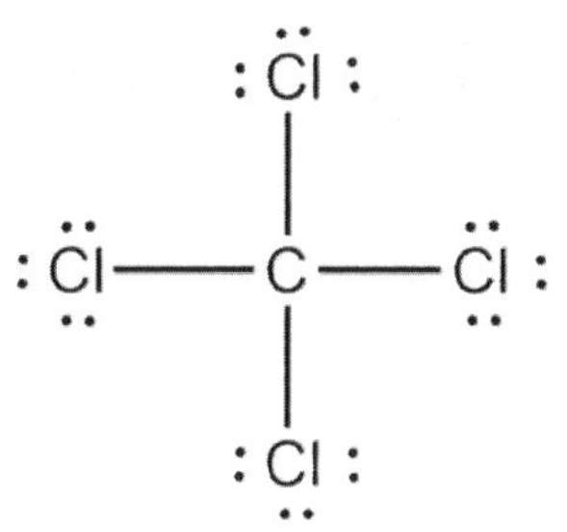

BF_3

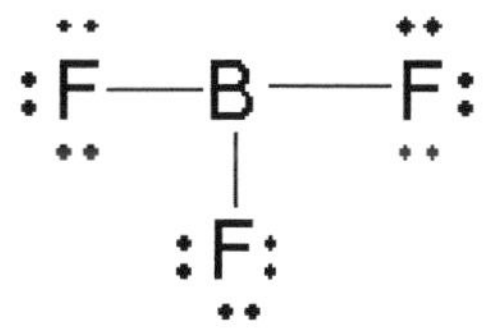

Resonance structures

For some molecules, more than one Lewis structure may be drawn due to the delocalization of electrons. In order to determine which resonance structure is the most stable, calculate the formal charge of each structure. The structure with the lowest formal charge is the most stable. The actual molecule is a hybrid of all the possible Lewis structures. An example of resonance occurs in benzene, C_6H_6. The two possible Lewis structures for benzene are shown below. The only difference between the two Lewis structures is the placement of the single and double bonds between the carbon atoms.

Studies show that in reality, neither Lewis structure is correct. In fact, all the bonds between the carbon atoms are exactly the same. The structure of the resonance hybrid of benzene is often represented by the drawing shown below. The circle inside the ring of carbons represents the delocalized electrons that are shared among all the carbon atoms of the ring.

Possible Lewis Structures -   Resonance Hybrid

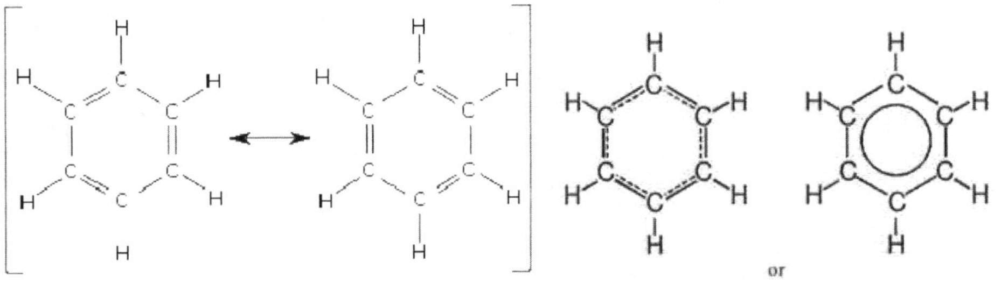

or

Molecular geometries

Linear — All diatomic molecules are linear molecules. Also, molecules with two bonding groups and two nonbonding pairs of electrons are linear. The bond angle measurement for linear molecules is 180°.

Trigonal planar — For a trigonal planar molecule, the central atom has three bonding pairs of electrons and zero nonbonding pairs. These molecules are an exception to the octet rule. The bond angle measurement for trigonal planar molecules is 120°.

Angular — For an angular molecule, the central atom has two bonding pairs of electrons and one or two nonbonding pairs. The bond angle measurement for angular molecules is less than 120° if there is one nonbonding pair, and less than 109° if there are two.

Tetrahedral — For a tetrahedral molecule, the central atom has four bonding pairs of electrons and zero nonbonding pairs. The bond angle measurement for tetrahedral molecules is 109.5°.

Trigonal pyramidal — For a trigonal pyramidal molecule, the central atom has three bonding pairs and one nonbonding pair. The bond angle measurement for trigonal pyramidal molecules is less than 109.5°.

<u>Examples</u>

Linear — Nitric oxide (NO) is another name for nitrogen monoxide. All diatomic molecules are linear.

Trigonal planar — Boron trifluoride (BF_3) has three bonding pairs and zero nonbonding pairs around the central atom. Therefore, boron trifluoride is trigonal planar.

Angular or bent — Oxygen difluoride (OF_2) has two bonding pairs and two nonbonding pairs around the central angle. Therefore, oxygen difluoride is angular or bent.

Tetrahedral — Methane (CH_4) has four bonding pairs and zero nonbonding pairs around the central angle. Therefore, methane is tetrahedral.

Ammonia — Ammonia (NH_3) has three bonding pairs and one bonding pair around the central atom. Therefore, ammonia is trigonal pyramidal.

Polar and nonpolar molecules

Covalently bonded molecules are either polar or nonpolar depending on the type and arrangement of their covalent bonds. Covalent bonds are polar if the electronegativities of the two atoms sharing the pair of electron differ. With differing electronegativities, the electrons are shared unequally with the pair of electrons displaced more toward the more electronegative atom. This results in a polar covalent bond. If the bonds are arranged symmetrically around a central atom, the polar bonds will "cancel" each other out resulting in a nonpolar molecule. If a molecule contains polar covalent bonds that are not arranged symmetrically in a way to "cancel" each other out, the molecule is polar. Molecules with only nonpolar covalent bonds are always nonpolar. Only molecules with polar covalent bonds can be polar.

Examples

> CH_4 — Nonpolar: Methane or CH_4 has a tetrahedral geometry with four hydrogen atoms covalently bonded around the central carbon atom. These four bonds are polar covalent bonds, but because they are arranged symmetrically around the central carbon atom, the molecule is nonpolar.

> CO_2 — Nonpolar: Carbon dioxide, or CO_2, is a linear molecule with two oxygen atoms covalently double bonded to a central carbon atom. These two double bonds are polar covalent bonds, but because they are arranged symmetrically around the carbon atom, the molecule is nonpolar.

> H_2S — Polar: Dihydrogen sulfide, or H_2S, is an angular molecule with the two hydrogen atoms covalently bonded to an oxygen atom. This molecule has two bonding pairs and one nonbonding pair. Because of the nonbonding pair, the molecule is bent or angular. Because the polar bonds do not cancel each other out in this arrangement, the molecule is polar.

Problems

> *Explain which intermolecular interactions are present in each of the following:*

> a. NH_3
> b. CH_4
> c. H_2S

> a. NH_3
> The intermolecular forces present in a sample of NH_3 are London forces and hydrogen bonds. London forces are present between all molecules. Hydrogen bonds are present between molecules with hydrogen covalently bonded to nitrogen, fluorine, and oxygen.

> b. CH_4
> The intermolecular forces present in a sample of CH_4 are only London forces. London forces are present between all molecules. Because CH_4 is a nonpolar molecular molecule, no dipole–dipole forces are present.

> c. H_2S
> The intermolecular forces present in a sample of H_2S are London forces and dipole–dipole forces. London forces are present between all molecules. Dipole–dipole forces are present between polar molecules, and because H_2S is a polar molecule, dipole–dipole forces are present.

Hydrogen bonding

Hydrogen bonding is a type of intermolecular force present between molecules containing hydrogen atoms covalently bonded to oxygen, fluorine, or nitrogen. Hydrogen bonding is the strongest of the intermolecular forces. When hydrogen from one molecule is near a highly electronegative atom such as oxygen, fluorine, or nitrogen in another molecule and acts as a bridge between another highly electronegative atom, a hydrogen bond is formed. Hydrogen bonding is responsible for the high boiling point in water and for the crystalline structure of ice.

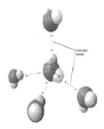

Dipole-induced dipole intermolecular forces

Whereas dipole–dipole intermolecular forces are between two polar molecules, a dipole-induced intermolecular force is between a polar molecule and a nonpolar molecule. Dipole-induced dipole intermolecular forces are forces that occur when a dipole induces a temporary dipole in a molecule that is nonpolar. The electron cloud of the nonpolar molecule is distorted when it comes near the electron cloud of a dipole. This is typically a weak intermolecular force. However, this dipole-induced dipole intermolecular force is responsible for the stability of hydrates formed from hydrocarbons and some of the noble gases.

Dipole–dipole intermolecular forces

Dipole–dipole forces are intermolecular forces that occur only between polar molecules. Polar molecules have positive and negative ends because of an unequal sharing of electrons due to the differences in electronegativities between the atoms of the molecules. The positive end of one molecule is attracted to the negative end of the other molecules. Dipole–dipole forces are stronger than London (dispersion) forces but weaker than hydrogen bonds. In the figure below, the dipole–dipole force between the positive end of one hydrogen chloride molecule and the negative end of another hydrogen chloride molecule is indicated by the dashed line.

$$\overset{\delta+}{H}\text{—}\overset{\delta-}{Cl}\text{- - - - -}\overset{\delta+}{H}\text{—}\overset{\delta-}{Cl}$$

London forces

London forces are intermolecular forces that exist between all molecules due to the temporary instantaneous dipoles induced by an unequal distribution of electrons around a molecule. London forces are present between all molecules of liquids, solids, and gases. London forces are the weakest of the intermolecular forces and the only intermolecular forces present between nonpolar molecules. London forces are also known as London dispersion forces or dispersion forces. London forces are weaker than both dipole–dipole forces and hydrogen bonds.

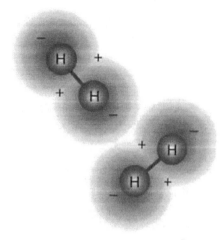

Properties affected by bonding and structure.

Bonding and structure determine whether a substance exists naturally as a solid, liquid, or gas. Properties that are affected by bonding and structure include boiling point, freezing point, and vapor pressure. Bonding and structure determine if a substance is soluble in water or in nonpolar solvents. Also affected are the viscosity of liquids and whether a solid material is hard or soft and whether or not a substance forms crystals or is amorphous. Bonding affects the conductivity of heat and electricity determining if a substance is a good insulator or conductor.

Boiling points and melting points

Bonding and structure affect boiling points and melting points. The types of bonds within molecules affect boiling and melting points. Compounds with ionic bonds typically have high melting and boiling points, whereas compounds with covalent bonds typically have low melting and boiling points. Intermolecular forces also affect these points. Substances with hydrogen bonds typically have high boiling and melting points. For example, hydrogen bonds are responsible for the high boiling and melting points of water. For example, the noble gases are indeed all gases.

Solubility

Bonding and structure affect solubility. The basic idea behind solubility is *like dissolves like*. This means that solutes with polar molecules typically dissolve in solvents with polar molecules. The polarity of the molecules is determined by the type of bonds and the arrangement of those bonds in the molecules. For example, both salt and table sugar (sucrose) dissolve in water because salt, table sugar, and water all have polar molecules. Solutes with nonpolar molecules typically dissolve in solvents with nonpolar molecules. For example, a grease stain will not rinse out with water because water consists of polar molecules due to the asymmetrical arrangement of the polar bonds and grease is a type of lipid that is nonpolar.

Equilibrium vapor pressure

Vapor pressure is related to the boiling point of a substance. The boiling point of a substance is the temperature at which the vapor pressure equals the atmospheric pressure. In general, as the vapor pressure increases, the boiling point decreases. Compounds with ionic bonds typically have high boiling points and low vapor pressures. Compounds with covalent bonds typically have low boiling points and high vapor pressures. Substances with the strongest intermolecular forces, hydrogen bonds, typically have high boiling points and low vapor pressures.

Energetics / Thermochemistry

Conservation of Energy and Matter

Law of conservation of energy

The law of conservation of energy states that in a closed system, energy cannot be created or destroyed but only changed from one form to another. This is also known as the first law of thermodynamics. Another way to state this is that the total energy in an isolated system is constant. Energy comes in many forms that may be transformed from one kind to another, but in a closed system, the total amount of energy is conserved or remains constant. For example, potential energy can be converted in kinetic energy, thermal energy, radiant energy, or mechanical energy. In an isolated chemical reaction, there can be no energy created or destroyed. The energy simply changes forms.

Law of conservation of mass

The law of conservation of mass is also known as the law of conservation of matter. This basically means that in a closed system, the total mass of the products must equal the total mass of the reactants. This could also be stated that in a closed system, mass never changes. A consequence of this law is that matter is never created or destroyed during a typical chemical reaction. The atoms of the reactants are simply rearranged to form the products. The number and type of each specific atom involved in the reactants is identical to the number and type of atoms in the products. This is the key principle used when balancing chemical equations. In a balanced chemical equation, the number of moles of each element on the reactant side equals the number of moles of each element on the product side.

Forms of Energy

Kinetic and potential energy

The internal energy of a system may be categorized as kinetic energy or potential energy. Kinetic energy is the energy of a system associated with movement. In chemical systems, this movement is predicted by the kinetic theory of matter and is due to the random movement of the particles that make up the system. The kinetic energy of a particle may be calculated by the following formula: $KE = \frac{1}{2}mv^2$, where KE is the kinetic energy in joules, m is the mass of the particle in kilograms, and v is the velocity of the particle in meters per second. Potential energy is the stored energy in a system associated with position or configuration. In chemical systems, this energy is the energy associated with the chemical bonds and intermolecular forces of the matter contained in the system.

Chemical, electrical, electromagnetic, nuclear, and thermal energy

Different types of energy may be associated with systems. Chemical energy is the energy that is stored in chemical bonds and intermolecular forces. Electrical energy is the energy associated with the movement of electrons or ions through a material. Electromagnetic energy is the energy of electromagnetic waves of several frequencies including radio waves, microwaves, infrared light, visible light, ultraviolet light, x-rays, and gamma rays. Nuclear energy is the binding energy that is stored within an atom's nucleus. Thermal energy is the total internal kinetic energy of a system due to the random motions of the particles.

Energy within chemical systems converted between forms

Chemical energy is the energy stored in molecules in the bonds between the atoms of those molecules and energy associated with the intermolecular forces. This stored potential energy may be converted into kinetic energy and then into heat. During a chemical reaction, atoms may be rearranged and chemical bonds may be formed or broken accompanied by a corresponding absorption or release of energy, usually in the form of heat. According to the first law of thermodynamics, during these energy conversions, the total amount of energy must be conserved.

Temperature and Thermal Energy

Temperature and temperature scales

Temperature is a measure of the average kinetic energy of the atoms or molecules in a system. The Celsius scale is the most commonly used scale with the freezing point of water at 0 °C and the boiling point of water at 100 °C. Normal body temperature is 37 °C. On the Fahrenheit scale, water freezes at 32 °F and boils at 212 °F. Normal body temperature is 98.6 °F. In chemistry, the Kelvin scale is frequently used. Water freezes at 273.15 K and boils at 373.15 K. The Celsius scale and the Kelvin scale have exactly 100 ° between the freezing point and boiling point of water. The Fahrenheit scale has 180 ° between the freezing point and the boiling point of water. The value of 1 °F is 100/180 or 5/9 of the size of 1 °C. The formulas to convert between the temperature scales are as follows:
$T_C = \frac{5}{9}(T_F - 32); \; T_F = \frac{9}{5}T_C + 32; \; T_K = T_C + 273.15.$

Problems

Perform the following temperature conversions.

1. Convert 200.0 °F to the Celsius scale.
2. Convert 24.0 °C to the Fahrenheit scale.
3. Convert 21.5 °C to the Kelvin scale.

1. To convert from 200.0 °F to °C, use the equation $T_C = \frac{5}{9}(T_F - 32)$.
Substituting 200.0 in for T_F yields $T_C = \frac{5}{9}(200.0 - 32) = \frac{5}{9}(168.0) = $ 93.33 °C.

2. To convert from 24.0 °C to °F, use the equation $T_F = \frac{9}{5}T_C + 32$. Substituting 24.0 in for T_C yields $T_F = $
$\frac{9}{5}(24.0) + 32 = 43.2 + 32 = 75.2$ °F.

3. To convert from 21.5 °C to K, use the equation $T_K = T_C + 273.15$.
Substituting 21.5 in for T_C yields $T_K = 21.5 + 273.15 = 294.7$ K.

Thermal energy and appropriate units

Thermal energy is part of a system's total internal energy, which consists of potential and kinetic energy. Thermal energy is the total internal kinetic energy of a system due to the random motions of the particles. The thermal energy of a system is measured by its temperature, which is the average kinetic energy of the particles in that system. The flow of thermal energy is referred to as heat. Appropriate units for thermal energy include the joule (J), British thermal unit (Btu) (1 Btu = 1,055 J), calorie (1 calorie = 4.1868 J), and Calorie (1 Calorie = 1 kilocalorie).

Heat transfer

Heat transfer is the flow of thermal energy, which is measured by temperature. Heat will flow from warmer objects to cooler objects until an equilibrium is reached in which both objects are at the same temperature. Because the particles of warmer objects possess a higher kinetic energy than the particles of cooler objects, the particles of the warmer objects are vibrating more quickly and collide more often, transferring energy to the cooler objects in which the particles have less kinetic energy and are moving more slowly. Heat may be transferred by conduction, convection, or radiation. In conduction, heat is transferred by direct contact between two objects. In convection, heat is transferred by moving currents. In radiation, heat is transferred by electromagnetic waves.

Example

> *Calculate the amount of heat lost by a piece of copper with a mass of 100.0 g when it cools from 100.0 °C to 20.0 °C. The specific heat of copper is 0.380 J/(g·°C).*
>
> To calculate the amount of heat lost by a piece of copper with a mass of 100.0 g when it cools from 100.0 °C to 20.0 °C, use the equation $Q = mc\Delta T$, where Q is the amount of heat lost in joules, m is the mass of the copper in grams, c is the specific heat of copper, and ΔT is the change in temperature $T_2 - T_1$ in degrees Celsius. Substituting 100.0 g for m, 0.380 J/(g·°C) for c, 20.0 °C for T_2, and 100.0 °C for T_1 yields $Q = (100.0 \text{ g})(0.380 \text{ J/(g·°C)})(20.0 \text{ °C} - 100.0 \text{ °C}) = -3{,}040$ J. The negative value confirms that heat was lost as the copper cooled.

Heat capacity and specific heat

Heat capacity is the amount of heat required to raise a sample of matter by 1 °C. Heat capacity is an extensive property and varies with the amount of matter in the sample. The greater the mass of the sample, the higher the heat capacity of the sample. This means that a specific type of matter will have different heat capacities depending on the size of the sample. Heat capacity may be represented by the formula $C = \dfrac{Q}{\Delta T}$, where Q is the heat in joules and ΔT is the change in temperature in degrees Celsius. Specific heat is the amount of heat required to raise the temperature of a unit mass by 1°. The formula for specific heat is

- 44 -

$c = \frac{Q}{m\Delta T}$, where Q is the heat in joules, ΔT is the change in temperature in degrees Celsius, and m is the mass of the sample. Because the specific heat formula incorporates the mass of the sample, a specific type of substance will have a constant specific heat, making specific heat an intensive property.

Calorimeter

The specific heat of a substance can be determined using a calorimeter. A known amount of the substance is heated to a known temperature. In the classroom setting, this can be accomplished by placing the metal in a loosely stoppered test tube and then placing the test tube in boiling water. The calorimeter is prepared by placing water of a known amount and temperature in the calorimeter. The heated metal is carefully placed into the water in the calorimeter. The temperature of the water is carefully monitored until it stops rising. The final temperature of the metal will be equal to the final temperature of the water. The heat lost by the metal equals the heat gained by the water as shown by the following equations:

$Q_{\text{lost by the metal}} = Q_{\text{gained by the water}}$
$-m_{\text{metal}} c_{\text{metal}} \Delta T_{\text{metal}} = m_{\text{water}} c_{\text{water}} \Delta T_{\text{water}}$,
where Q is the amount of heat lost or gained in joules, m is the mass in grams, c is the specific heat, and ΔT is the change in temperature $T_2 - T_1$ in degrees Celsius.

Calorimetry problem

In a calorimetry experiment, to determine the specific heat of an unknown metal with a mass of 100.0 g, the temperature of the unknown metal dropped 20.0° C. The temperature of the water with a mass of 100.0 g in the calorimeter raised 1.00 °C.

Explain how to find the specific heat of the unknown metal. Use 4.20 J/(g·°C) for the specific heat of water.

The heat lost by the metal must equal the heat gained by the water as shown in the equation
$Q_{\text{lost by metal}} = Q_{\text{gained by the water}}$, where Q is the amount of heat lost or gained in joules. To calculate the specific heat of the metal, use the equation $-m_{\text{metal}}$
$c_{\text{metal}} \Delta T_{\text{metal}} = m_{\text{water}} c_{\text{water}} \Delta T_{\text{water}}$,
where m is the mass of the metal or water in grams, c is the specific heat of the metal or water, and ΔT is the change in temperature $(T_2 - T_1)$ in degrees Celsius in the metal or water. Solving the equation for c_{metal} results in $c_{\text{metal}} = -\frac{m_{\text{water}} c_{\text{water}} \Delta T_{\text{water}}}{m_{\text{metal}} \Delta T_{\text{metal}}}$. Substituting in the given information yields $c_{\text{metal}} = -\frac{(100.0 \text{ g})(4.20 \text{ J/g·°C})(1.00 \text{ °C})}{(100.0 \text{ g})(20.0 \text{ °C})} = 0.21 \text{ J/g·°C}$.

Phase Transitions

Phase diagram and critical point

A phase diagram is a graph or chart of pressure versus temperature that represents the solid, liquid, and gaseous phases of a substance and the transitions between these phases. Typically, pressure is located on the vertical axis, and temperature is located along the horizontal axis. The curves drawn on the graph represent points at which different phases are in an equilibrium state. These curves indicate at which pressure and temperature the phase changes of sublimation, melting, and boiling occur. Specifically, the curve between the liquid and gas phases indicates the pressures and temperatures at which the liquid and gas phases are in equilibrium. The curve between the solid and liquid phases indicates the temperatures and pressures at which the solid and liquid phases are in equilibrium. The open spaces on the graph represent the distinct phases solid, liquid, and gas. The point on the curve at which the graph splits is referred to as the *critical point*. At the critical point, the solid, liquid, and gas phases all exist in a state of equilibrium.

Lettered regions of a phase diagram

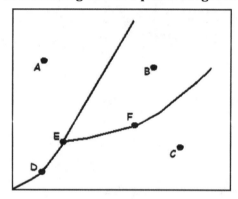

A—Solid phase: This is a region of high pressure and low temperature where the substance always exists as a solid.
B—Liquid phase: This is a region of pressure and temperature where the substance is in the liquid phase.
C—Gas phase: This is a region of pressure and temperature where the substance is in the gaseous phase.
D—Sublimation point: The portion of the curve that contains point D shows all the combinations of pressure and temperature at which the solid phase is in equilibrium with the gaseous phase.
E—Critical point: The point at which the solid, liquid, and gaseous phases are all in equilibrium.
F—Boiling point: The line that contains point F indicates all the combinations of pressure and temperature at which the liquid phase and gas phase are in equilibrium.

Heat of vaporization, heat of fusion, and heat of sublimation

The *heat of vaporization* (ΔH_{vap}) is the amount of heat that must be added to one mole of a substance to change the substance from the liquid phase to the gaseous phase.

The *heat of fusion* (ΔH_{fus}) is the amount of heat that must be added to one mole of a substance to change the substance from the solid phase to the liquid phase.
The *heat of sublimation* (ΔH_{sub}) is the amount of heat that must be added to one mole of a substance to change the substance directly from the solid phase to the gaseous phase without passing through the liquid phase.

Problem #1

> *Calculate the amount of heat required to change 100.0 g of ice at –10.0 °C to water at 10.0 °C. (ΔH_{fus} = 334 J/g; c_{water} = 4.18 J/(g·°C), c_{ice} = 2.06 J/(g·°C)).*

> To calculate the amount of heat required to change 100.0 g of ice at –10.0 °C to water at 10.0 °C, it is necessary to calculate the heat required for each step along the way. Step 1 is to calculate the heat required to raise the temperature of the ice from –10.0 °C to 0.0 °C. Step 2 is to calculate the amount of heat required to melt the ice. Finally, step 3 is to calculate the amount of heat required to raise the temperature of the water from 0.0 °C to 10.0 °C. For steps 1 and 3, the required equation is $Q = mc\Delta T$. Because step 2 is a phase change, the required equation is $Q = m\Delta H_{fus}$. For step 1: $Q_1 =$ (100.0 g)(2.06 J/(g·°C))(0.0 °C – (–10.0 °C)) = 2,060 J. For step 2: $Q_2 = m\Delta H_{fus}$ = (100.0 g)(334 J/g) = 33,400 J. For step 3: Q_1 = (100.0 g)(4.18 J/(g·°C))(10.0 °C – 0.0 °C) = 4,180 J. Adding $Q_1 + Q_2 + Q_3$ = 2,060 J + 33,400 J + 4,180 J = 39,640 J.

Problem #2

> *Calculate the amount of heat required to change 100.0 g of water at 90.0 °C to steam at 110.0 °C (ΔH_{vap} = 2,260 J/g; c_{steam} = 1.86 J/(g·°C), c_{water} = 4.18 J/(g·°C)).*

> To calculate the amount of heat required to change 100.0 g of water at 90.0 °C to steam at 110.0 °C, it is necessary to calculate the heat required at each step along the way. Step 1 is to calculate the heat required to raise the temperature of the water from 90.0 °C to 100.0 °C. Step 2 is to calculate the amount of heat required to change the water to steam. Finally, step 3 is to calculate the amount of heat required to raise the temperature of the steam from 100.0 °C to 110.0 °C. For steps 1 and 3, the required equation is $Q = mc\Delta T$. Because Step 2 is a phase change, the required equation is $Q = m\Delta H_{vap}$. For step 1: Q_1 = (100.0 g)(4.18 J/(g·°C))(100.0 °C – 90.0 °C) = 4,180 J. For step 2: $Q_2 = m\Delta H_{vap}$ = (100.0 g)(2,260 J/g) = 226,000 J. For step 3: Q_1 = (100.0 g)(1.86 J/(g·°C))(110.0 °C – 100.0 °C) = 1,860 J. Adding $Q_1 + Q_2 + Q_3$ = 4,180 J + 226,000 J + 1,860 J = 233,040 J.

Heating curve of water from –10 °C to 110 °C

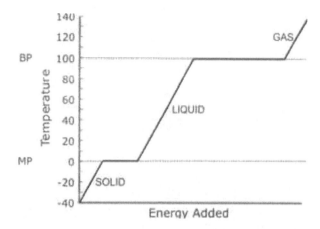

In the first portion of the curve, the graph slants up and to the right as the ice is a solid that is increasing in temperature from –10 °C to 0 °C. In the second portion of the curve, the graph remains horizontal during the phase change from solid to liquid as the temperature remains constant at 0 °C. In the third portion of the curve, the graph slants up and to the right as the water now is in the liquid state and is increasing in temperature from 0 °C to 100 °C. In the fourth portion of the curve, the graph remains horizontal during the phase change from liquid to gas as the temperature remains at 100 °C. In the last portion of the curve, the graph slants up and to the right as water now is the gaseous state and the steam is increasing in temperature from 100 °C to 110 °C.

Calculate the amount of heat required during each portion of the heating curve.

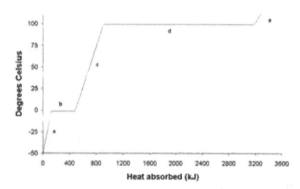

For portion a, $Q = mc_{ice}\Delta T$, where Q is the amount of heat gained in joules, m is the mass of the ice in grams, c is the specific heat of ice, and ΔT is the change in temperature in degrees Celsius.

For portion b, $Q = m\Delta H_{fus}$, where Q is the amount of heat gained in joules, m is the mass of the ice/water in grams, and ΔH_{fus} is the heat of fusion for water in joules/gram.

For portion c, $Q = mc_{water}\Delta T$, where Q is the amount of heat gained in joules, m is the mass of the water in grams, c is the specific heat of water, and ΔT is the change in temperature in degrees Celsius.

- 48 -

For portion d, $Q = m\Delta H_{vap}$, where Q is the amount of heat gained in joules, m is the mass of the water/steam in grams, and ΔH_{vap} is the heat of fusion for water in joules/gram.

For portion e, $Q = mc_{steam}\Delta T$, where Q is the amount of heat gained in joules, m is the mass of the steam in grams, c is the specific heat of steam, and ΔT is the change temperature in degrees Celsius.

Energetics of Chemical Reactions / Laws of Thermodynamics

Exothermic and endothermic reactions

Exothermic reactions release heat energy, whereas endothermic reactions absorb energy. Exothermic reactions can be represented by reactants → products + heat. Endothermic reactions can be represented by reactants + heat → products. The change in enthalpy for exothermic reactions is positive, whereas the change in enthalpy for endothermic reactions is negative. An example of an exothermic reaction is the burning of propane. An example of an endothermic reaction is the reaction that takes place in a first-aid cold pack.

Hess's law

Bond energy is the energy needed to break or form a bond. Hess's law can be used to calculate bond energy. Usually, Hess's law is used to state the relationship between the enthalpies of formations of the reactants and the enthalpies of formation of the products of a reaction. Basically, Hess's law states that when reactants are converted to products, the total sum of the energy required to break the bonds of the reactants minus the total sum of energy required to form the bonds of the products is equal to the heat of the reaction. Enthalpies of formation are generally used in place of the actual bond energies because enthalpies of formation have been standardized whereas the bond energies of individual molecules vary. Hess's law is given by the equation $\Delta H_{reaction}^{\circ} = \Sigma \Delta H_{f(products)}^{\circ} - \Sigma \Delta H_{f(reactants)}^{\circ}$.

<u>Problem</u>

Calculate the ΔH° for the following reaction: $3\ H_2\ (g) + N_2\ (g) \rightarrow 2\ NH_3\ (g)$ (ammonia: $\Delta H_f^{\circ} = -46.19\ kJ/mol$).

To calculate the ΔH° for the following reaction: $3\ H_2\ (g) + N_2\ (g) \rightarrow 2\ NH_3\ (g)$ given that for ammonia $\Delta H_f^{\circ} = -46.19$ kJ/mol, use the equation given by Hess's law: $\Delta H_{reaction}^{\circ} = \Sigma \Delta H_{f(products)}^{\circ} - \Sigma \Delta H_{f(reactants)}^{\circ}$. Recall that the enthalpy of formation (ΔH_f°) of an element in its uncombined state is zero. The number of moles of each reactant and product is the coefficients from the balanced chemical equation. Substituting this information and the given information into the equation yields $\Delta H_{reaction}^{\circ} = \Sigma \Delta H_{f(products)}^{\circ} - \Sigma \Delta H_{f(reactants)}^{\circ} = [(2\ mol)(-46.19\ kJ/mol)] - [(3\ mol)(0\ kJ/mol) + (1\ mol)(0\ kJ/mol)] = -92.38$ kJ.

Laws of thermodynamics

The zeroth law of thermodynamics describes the heat flow between three systems. If two systems are in equilibrium with a third system, then those two systems are in equilibrium with each other. The first law of thermodynamics describes the internal energy of a system in relation to the heat and work added and or removed from that system. The first law of thermodynamics is represented by the equation $\Delta E = q + w$, where ΔE is the change in internal energy, q is the heat added to the system, and w is the work done on the system.

The second law of thermodynamics describes the entropy of a system in relation to absolute temperature. The second law of thermodynamics is represented by the equation $\Delta S = \frac{Q}{T}$, where ΔS is the change in entropy of the system, Q is the heat added or removed from the system, and T is the absolute temperature.

The Third law of thermodynamics describes the entropy of crystals at extremely low temperatures. The entropy of a pure crystal approaches zero as the temperature of the crystal approaches absolute zero.

Spontaneous/reversible processes

Some chemical processes are spontaneous. According to the second law of thermodynamics, systems or processes always tend to a state of greater entropy or lower potential energy. Some exothermic chemical systems are spontaneous because they can increase their stability by reaching a lower potential energy. If processes or reactions have products at a lower potential energy, these processes tend to be spontaneous. Spontaneous reactions have only one direction as given by the second law of thermodynamics. Spontaneous processes go in the direction of greater entropy and lower potential energy. To be reversible, a reaction or process has to be able to go back and forth the between two states. A spontaneous process is irreversible.

Change in enthalpy in chemical/physical processes

All chemical processes involve either the release or the absorption of heat. Enthalpy is this heat energy. Enthalpy is a state function that is equivalent to the amount of heat a system exchanges with its surroundings. For exothermic processes, which release heat, the change in enthalpy (ΔH) is negative because the final enthalpy is less than the initial enthalpy. For endothermic processes, which absorb heat, the change in enthalpy (ΔH) is positive because the final enthalpy is greater than the initial enthalpy.

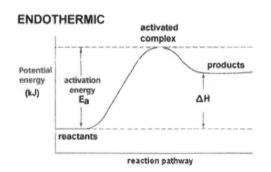 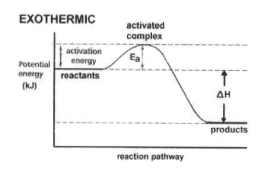

Gibbs energy

Gibbs energy (G), also known as Gibbs free energy, is the energy of the system that is available to do work. Gibbs energy determines the spontaneity of chemical and physical processes. Some processes are spontaneous because $\Delta H < 0$ or because $\Delta S > 0$. If one of the conditions is favorable but the other condition is not favorable, Gibbs energy can be used to determine if a process is spontaneous. Gibbs energy is given by $G = H - TS$. For processes that occur at constant temperature, $\Delta G = \Delta H - T\Delta S$. If ΔG is equal to zero, then the reaction is at equilibrium and neither the forward nor the reverse reaction is spontaneous. If ΔG is less than zero, then the forward reaction is spontaneous. If ΔG is greater than zero, then the reverse reaction is spontaneous.

Entropy

Entropy (S) is the amount of disorder or randomness of a system. According to the second law of thermodynamics, systems tend toward a state of greater entropy. The second law of thermodynamics can also be stated as $\Delta S > 0$. Processes with positive changes in entropy tend to be spontaneous. For example, melting is a process with a positive ΔS. When a solid changes into a liquid state, the substance becomes more disordered; therefore, entropy increases. Entropy also will increase in a reaction in which the number of moles of gases increases due to the amount of disorder increasing. Entropy increases when a solute dissolves into a solvent due to the increase in the number of particles. Entropy increases when a system is heated due to the particles moving faster and the amount of disorder increasing.

Chemical Kinetics

Chemical kinetics

Chemical kinetics is the study of the rates or speeds of chemical reactions and the various factors that affect these rates or speeds. The rate or speed of a reaction is the change in concentration of the reactant(s) or product(s) per unit of time. Another way to state this is that chemical kinetics is study of the rate of change of the concentrations of the reactant(s) and product(s) and the factors that affect that rate of change. The study of catalysts is part of chemical kinetics. Catalysts are substances that speed up the rate of reactions without being consumed. Examples of reactions that occur at different rates include the explosion of trinitrotoluene (TNT), which occurs at a very fast rate, compared to the burning of a log, which occurs at a much slower rate.

Example

> Give the rate law for this general reaction: $aA + bB + cC \ldots \rightarrow$ products.

The rate of a chemical reaction can be defined as the following:
- $\text{rate} = \dfrac{\text{change in concentration}}{\text{change in time}}$.

This is usually represented by a rate law. The rate law for the general reaction $aA + bB + cC \ldots \rightarrow$ products is given by rate $= k[A]^x[B]^y[C]^z$, where k is the rate constant; $[A]$, $[B]$, and $[C]$ represent the concentrations of the reactants; and x, y, and z represent the reaction orders. The exponents x, y, and z must be experimentally determined. They do not necessarily equal the coefficients from the balanced chemical equation.

Activation energy

Activation energy is the minimum amount of energy that must be possessed by reactant atoms or molecules in order to react. This is due to the fact that it takes a certain amount of energy to break bonds or form bonds between atoms. Reactants lacking the activation energy required will not be able to perform the necessary breaking or forming of bonds regardless of how often they collide. Catalysts lower the activation energy of a reaction and therefore increase the rate of reaction.

Reaction mechanism

Often, when studying specific reactions, only the net reactions are given. Realistically, reactions take place in a series of steps or elementary reactions as shown in the reaction mechanism. Reaction mechanisms show how a reaction proceeds in a series of steps. Some steps are slow, and some are fast. Each step has its own reaction mechanism. The slowest step in the reaction mechanism coincides with the step with the greatest activation energy. This step is known as the rate-determining step.

Catalyst

A catalyst is a chemical that accelerates or speeds up a chemical reaction without being consumed or used up in the reaction. Although catalysts are not consumed or permanently changed during the process of the reaction, catalysts do participate in the elementary reaction of the reaction mechanisms. Catalysts cannot make an impossible reaction take place, but catalysts do greatly increase the rate of a reaction. Catalysts lower the activation energy. Because the activation energy is the minimum energy required for molecules to react, lowering the activation energy makes it possible for more of the reactant molecules to react.

Factors that affect reaction rate

Factors that affect reaction rate include concentration, surface area, and temperature. Increasing the concentration of the reactants increases the number of collisions between those reactants and therefore increases the reaction rate. Increasing the surface area of contact between the reactants also increases the number of collisions and therefore increases the reaction rate. Finally, increasing the temperature of the reactants increases the number of collisions but more significantly also increases the kinetic energy of the reactants, which in turn increases the fraction of molecules meeting activation energy requirement. With more molecules at the activation energy, more of the reactants are capable of completing the reaction.

Equilibrium

Chemical Reaction Equilibrium

Chemical equilibrium

A chemical equilibrium occurs when a reaction is reversible and the rate of the forward reaction equals the rate of the reverse reaction. The forward and reverse reactions are continually occurring, but the individual concentration of the reaction and the products do not change. The concentration of the reactants and products are not necessarily equal to each other. For this to occur, the reaction must take place in a closed system in which none of the reactants or products can escape and in which no heat is added or lost.

Problem #1
Writing an equilibrium constant expression from a given equilibrium equation

Given the following equilibrium reaction: $aA + bB + \ldots \leftrightarrow cC + dD$, the equilibrium constant is calculated by the expression $k = \frac{[C]^c[D]^d}{[A]^a[B]^b}$. The brackets indicate "the concentration of" each individual reactant and product. The coefficients from the balanced chemical equation are used for the exponents in the equilibrium constant expression. Pure liquids and pure solids are not represented in the equilibrium constants. The concentration of gases and the concentration of solutes do appear in the expressions for equilibrium constants. Note that the concentrations of the products are in the numerator and the concentrations of the reactant are in the denominator.

Problem #2
Write equilibrium constant expressions for each of the following equilibriums:

1. $2SO_2$ (g) + O_2 (g) $\leftrightarrow$ $2SO_3$ (g).
2. $CaCO_3$ (s) $\leftrightarrow$ CaO (s) + CO_2 (g).
3. CaH_2 (s) + $2H_2O$ (l) $\leftrightarrow$ $Ca(OH)_2$ (aq) + $2H_2$ (g).
4. H^+ (aq) + OH^- (aq) $\leftrightarrow$ H_2O (l).

1. All of the reactants and products are gases and need to be represented in the equilibrium constant. The concentration of the product is placed in the numerator, and the concentrations of the reactants are placed in the denominator. The coefficients from the balanced chemical equation are the exponents:

- $k = \frac{[SO_3]^2}{[SO_2]^2[O_2]}$.

2. The solid reactant $CaCO_3$ and the solid product CaO are not part of the equilibrium constant. The concentration of the gaseous product CO_2 is represented in the numerator.

- $k = [CO_2]$.

3. The solid reactant CaH_2 and the liquid reactant H_2O are not part of the equilibrium constant. Both products should be represented. The "2" coefficient of the gaseous hydrogen is the exponent on the concentration of the gaseous H_2.

- $k = [Ca(OH)_2][H_2]^2$.

4. Pure liquids are not represented in the equilibrium constant. Aqueous solutions are included in the equilibrium constant.

- $k = \dfrac{1}{[H^+][OH^-]}$.

Le Châtelier's principle

Le Châtelier's principle states that when a stressor is applied to a system in equilibrium, the system will respond in such a way to at least partially offset the stressor. Stressors include increasing or decreasing the temperature, increasing or decreasing the concentration of a reactant or product, and increasing or decreasing the pressure. Systems are described as "shifting left" or "shifting right" when a stressor is applied. For example, if the temperature is increased in an equilibrium in which the forward reaction is endothermic, the system will "shift right" in order to "use up" the heat that was applied. Increasing or decreasing the pressure of an equilibrium will only cause the equilibrium to "shift" if the number of moles of gases of the reactants differs from the number of moles of gases of the products. If there are no gases in the equilibrium or if the number of moles of gases of the reactants and products is equal, the change in pressure will have no effect on the equilibrium.

<u>Example #1</u>

Given the following equilibrium system, explain the effect of increasing the pressure on the production of ammonia:

$3H_2(g) + N_2(g) \leftrightarrow 2NH_3(g) \Delta H = -92$ kJ/mol.

Le Châtelier's principle states that when a stressor is applied to a system in equilibrium, the system will respond in such a way to at least partially offset the stressor. An increase or decrease in pressure will only affect an equilibrium if the number of moles of gases of the reactants differs from the number of moles of gases of the products. In this equilibrium, the total number of moles of gases of the reactants of the forward reaction is 4 moles, and the number of moles of gases of the products of the forward reaction is 2 moles. To offset an increase in pressure, the equilibrium will "shift" to the side with the lesser number of moles of gases to relieve that pressure. This equilibrium "shifts right" or from 4 moles of gas to 2 moles of gas. When the equilibrium shifts right, the concentration of ammonia in the equilibrium increases, resulting in an increase in the production of ammonia.

<u>Example #2</u>

> *Given the following equilibrium system, explain the effect of increasing the temperature on the production of ammonia:*

$$3H_2(g) + N_2(g) \leftrightarrow 2NH_3(g) \Delta H = -92 \text{ kJ/mol.}$$

Le Châtelier's principle states that when a stressor is applied to a system in equilibrium, the system will respond in such a way to at least partially offset the stressor. Because the forward reaction of the equilibrium is exothermic ($\Delta H < 0$), the reaction can be written as $3H_2(g) + N_2(g) \leftrightarrow 2NH_3(g) + $ heat. According to Le Châtelier's principle, the system will shift to offset or "use up" that heat. In this scenario, the equilibrium "shifts left." With a "shift to the left," more ammonia is "used up" as a reactant in the reverse reaction resulting in the overall production of ammonia decreasing.

Equilibrium in Ionic Solutions

Solubility of ionic compounds in water

If an ionic compound is soluble in water, the cations and anions will separate from each other when combined with water. In general, the rule for solubility is "like dissolves like." However, some ionic compounds are not soluble in water because the forces joining the ions are stronger than the intermolecular forces between the ions and the water molecules. Some general guidelines regarding solubility include the following: All nitrates and acetates are soluble. All chlorides, bromides, and iodides are soluble except those of silver, mercury(I), and lead(II). All sulfates are soluble except those of strontium, barium, mercury(I), and lead(II). All sulfides are insoluble except those of ammonium, the alkali metal cations, calcium, strontium, and barium. All carbonates are insoluble except those of ammonium and the alkali metal cations. All phosphates are insoluble except those of ammonium and the alkali metal cations. All hydroxides are insoluble except those of the alkali metal cations and calcium, strontium, and barium.

Soluble Ionic Compounds		Important Exceptions
Compounds containing	NO_3^-	None
	$C_2H_3O_2^-$	None
	Cl^-	Compounds of Ag^+, Hg_2^{2+}, and Pb^{2+}
	Br^-	Compounds of Ag^+, Hg_2^{2+}, and Pb^{2+}
	I^-	Compounds of Ag^+, Hg_2^{2+}, and Pb^{2+}
	SO_4^-	Compounds of Sr^{2+}, Ba^{2+}, Hg_2^{2+}, and Pb^{2+}
Insoluble Ionic Compounds		**Important Exceptions**
	S^{2-}	Compounds of NH_4^+, the alkali metal cations, and Ca^{2+}, Sr^{2+}, and Ba^{2+}
	CO_3^{2-}	Compounds of NH_4^+ and the alkali metal cations
	PO_4^{3-}	Compounds of NH_4^+ and the alkali metal cations
	OH^-	Compounds of the alkali metal cations, and Ca^{2+}, Sr^{2+}, and Ba^{2+}

Calculating K_{sp} and percent dissociation

The solubility product constant, K_{sp}, is the equilibrium constant for a solution equilibrium. If a general chemical equation for a solution equilibrium is given by ionic compound (s) $\leftrightarrow$ cation (aq) + anion (aq), then the solubility product constant K_{sp} = [cation][anion]. The percent dissociation for each ion is calculated by the following formula: percent dissociation $= \frac{\text{amount dissociated}}{\text{initial concentration}} \times 100\ \%$, where the amount dissociated in the molarity of the ion in solution and the initial concentration is the molarity of the original compound. In general, the more dilute a solution, the greater the percent dissociation.

<u>Example</u>

> *Calculate the solubility of AgBr if the solubility product constant, K_{sp}, for AgBr is 4.9×10^{-13} at 25 °C.*

> The dissociation reaction for AgBr can be written as AgBr (s) $\leftrightarrow$ Ag⁺ (aq) + Br⁻ (aq).

> Because the dissociation of AgBr produces equal moles of Ag⁺ and Br⁻ ions, the solubility is simply the concentration of the Ag⁺ ions, [Ag⁺], or the concentration of the Br⁻ ions, [Br⁻]. The solubility product constant for this reaction is given by K_{sp} = [Ag⁺][Br⁻], but because [Ag⁺] = [Br⁻], this can be written as K_{sp} = [Ag⁺]². Substituting in the given value for K_{sp} yields 4.9×10^{-13} = [Ag⁺]². Therefore, [Ag⁺] = 7.0×10^{-7} M. Finally, the solubility of AgBr is 7.0×10^{-7} M.

Common ion effect

The common ion effect is the decrease in the solubility of a salt in an electrolyte when that electrolyte solution already has an ion in common with that salt. An example of the common ion effect is when sodium chloride, NaCl, is dissolved in an aqueous solution of hydrochloric acid, HCl. The ions of the NaCl are Na⁺ and Cl⁻, and the ions of the HCl solution are H⁺ and Cl⁻. Therefore, the solute NaCl and the aqueous solution HCl share a common Cl⁻ ion. The equilibrium of the aqueous HCl solution can be represented by the following equation: HCl (g) + H_2O (l) $\leftrightarrow$ H_3O^+ (aq) + Cl⁻ (aq).

According to Le Châtelier's principle, when a stressor is applied to this equilibrium, the system will respond in such a way to at least partially offset the stressor. Adding the NaCl to this equilibrium increases the concentration of the Cl⁻ ions in solution, which would shift to the equilibrium to the left. The overall effect is that less Cl⁻ goes into solution. Therefore, because the solute and the solution share a common ion, the common ion effect is shown as the decrease in the solubility of the Cl⁻ ions.

Electrolytes and nonelectrolytes

Electrolytes are substances that dissociate in solution to form ions. Strong electrolytes ionize essentially completely. Weak electrolytes only ionize partially and form only a few ions in solution. Nonelectrolytes do not dissociate or form ions in solution. Strong electrolytes such as salt water, NaCl (aq), or hydrochloric acid, HCl (aq), are good conductors of electricity. Weak electrolytes such as acetic acid, $HC_2H_2O_2$ (aq), and ammonia, NH_3 (aq), are poor conductors of electricity. Nonelectrolytes such as sugar water, $C_{12}H_{22}O_{11}$ (aq), and ethanol, C_2H_5OH (aq), do not conduct electricity.

Acids and Bases

Properties of Acids and Bases

Acids and bases

Several differences exist between acids and bases. Acidic solutions tend to taste sour, whereas basic solutions tend to taste bitter. Dilute bases tend to feel slippery, whereas dilute acids feel like water. Active metals such as magnesium and zinc react with acids to produce hydrogen gas, but active metals usually do not react with bases. Acids and bases form electrolytes in aqueous solutions and conduct electricity. Acids turn blue litmus red, but bases turn red litmus blue. Acidic solutions have a pH of less than 7, whereas basic solutions have a pH of greater than 7.

Arrhenius acid and base

Arrhenius acids are substances that produce hydrogen ions (H^+) when dissolved in water to form aqueous solutions. Arrhenius bases are substances that produce hydroxide ions (OH^-) when dissolved in water to form aqueous solutions. The Arrhenius concept is limited to acids and bases in aqueous solutions and cannot be applied to other solids, liquids, and gases. Examples of Arrhenius acids include hydrochloric acid (HCl) and sulfuric acid (H_2SO_4). Examples of Arrhenius bases include sodium hydroxide (NaOH) and magnesium hydroxide ($Mg(OH)_2$).

Brønsted–Lowry acid and base

The Brønsted–Lowry concept is based on the donation or the acceptance of a proton. According to the Brønsted–Lowry concept, an acid is a substance that donates one or more protons to another substance and a base is a substance that accepts a proton from another substance. The Brønsted–Lowry concept can be applied to substances other than aqueous solutions. This concept is much broader than the Arrhenius concept, which can only be applied to aqueous solutions. The Brønsted–Lowry concept states that a substance cannot act like an acid (donate its proton) unless another substance is available to act as a base (accept the donated proton). In this concept, water may act as either an acid or a base. Hydrochloric acid (HCl) is an example of a Brønsted–Lowry acid. Ammonia (NH_3) is an example of a Brønsted–Lowry base.

Lewis acid and base

A Lewis acid is any substance that can accept a pair of nonbonding electrons. A Lewis base is any substance that can donate a pair of nonbonding electrons. According to the Lewis theory, all cations such as Mg^{2+} and Cu^{2+} are Lewis acids. Trigonal planar molecules, which are exceptions to the octet rule such as BF_3, are Lewis acids. Molecules such as CO_2 that have multiple bonds between two atoms that differ in electronegativities are Lewis acids, also. According to the Lewis theory, all anions such as OH^- are Lewis bases. Other examples of Lewis bases include trigonal pyramidal molecules such as ammonia, NH_3, and nonmetal oxides such as carbon monoxide, CO. Some compounds such as water, H_2O, can be either Lewis acids or bases.

Chemical equation for a neutralization reaction

Neutralization is a reaction of an acid and a base that yields a salt and water. The salt is formed from the cation of the base and the anion of the acid. The water is formed from the cation of the acid and the anion of the base: acid + base → salt + water

An example is the neutralization reaction of hydrochloric acid and sodium hydroxide to form sodium chloride and water:
- HCl (aq) + NaOH (aq) → NaCl (s) + H₂O (l).

Equivalence point

The *equivalence point* is by definition the point in a titration at which the analyte is neutralized. When the acid–base indicator starts to change color, the equivalence point has been reached. At this point, equivalent amounts of acids and bases have reacted. Also, at this point, [H⁺] = [OH⁻]. On an acid–base titration curve, the slope of the curve increases dramatically at the equivalence point. For strong acids and bases, the equivalence point occurs at a pH of 7. The figures below show the equivalence points for a strong acid titrated with a strong base (a) and a strong base titrated with a strong acid (b).

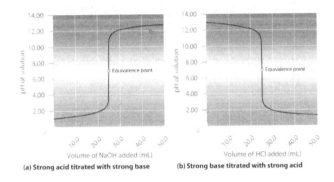

(a) Strong acid titrated with strong base   (b) Strong base titrated with strong acid

pH Scale

pH scale

The pH scale categorizes the acidity or alkalinity (basicity) of a solution. The pH value may be calculated by the formula pH = −log[H⁺], where [H⁺] is the concentration of hydrogen ions. The pH scales ranges from 0 to 14 with pH values near zero indicating the strongest acids and pH values near 14 indicating the strongest bases. With the pH scale, any solution with a pH < 7 is considered an acid and any solution with a pH > 7 is considered a base. Solutions with a pH of 7 are considered to be neutral.

pH and pOH

The pH of a solution may be calculated using the formula pH = −log[H⁺], where [H⁺] is the concentration of hydrogen ions. The pOH of a solution may be calculated using the formula pH = –log[OH⁻], where [OH⁻] is the concentration of hydroxide ions. The sum of the pH of a solution and the pOH of a solution is always 14. The pH of this HCl solution may be calculated using the formula pH = –log[0.0010 M] = 3. The sum of the pH and pOH is always 14. Therefore, the pOH may be calculated by the formula 14 – 3 = 11.

Example

> Calculate [H⁺] and [OH⁻] when given the pH or pOH. Given a solution with a pOH of 8.2, explain how to calculate pH, [H⁺], and [OH⁻].
>
> Because pH = –log[H⁺], the [H⁺] may be calculated by [H⁺] = antilog (–pH). Because pOH = –log[OH⁻], the [OH⁻] may be calculated by [OH⁻] = antilog (–pOH). Also, because the pH + pOH = 14, the pOH may be calculated by the formula 14 – pH = pOH. For example, given a solution with a pOH pf 8.0, the [OH⁻] = antilog (–8.0) = 1.0×10^{-8}. The pH = 14 – 8.0 = 6.0. The [H⁺] = antilog (–6.0) = 1×10^{-6}.

K_w

Pure water dissociates to a very small extent and reaches this equilibrium: $H_2O(l) + H_2O(l) \leftrightarrow H_3O^+ (aq) + OH^- (aq)$. The equilibrium constant for this equilibrium is called the ion product constant of water, or K_w. The constant K_w can be represented by $K_w = [H_3O^+][OH^-]$. The reactant H_2O is not represented in the equilibrium expression because it is essentially a pure liquid. The ion product constant of water K_w varies with temperature. As temperature increases, K_w increases and pH decreases. Therefore, this constant must be given at a specific temperature. At 25 °C, $[H_3O^+] = [OH^-] = 1 \times 10^{-7}$ M, which corresponds to pure water being neutral with a pH of 7.

Acid-Base Titrations

Acid–base indicators

Acid–base indicators are one method to determine the range of the pH of a solution. Acid–base indicators change with the pH of the solution and are less precise than using a pH meter. However, acid–base indicators are used to indicate the completion of a titration to determine the concentration of an acidic or basic solution. Examples of acid–base indicators include methyl violet, litmus, and phenolphthalein. Methyl violet turns from yellow to blue with a pH range of 0.0–1.6. Litmus turns from red to blue with a pH range of 4.5–8.3. Phenolphthalein turns from colorless to reddish purple with a pH range of 8.3–10.0.

Endpoint in a titration

During a titration, when the acid–base indicator has fully changed color, the endpoint has been reached. If the proper acid–base indicator with the correct pH range has been used, this should also correspond to the equivalence point. For example, if trying to determine the pH of an unknown base using phenolphthalein, the solution should change from colorless to pink at the equivalence point. If trying to determine the pH of an unknown acid using methyl violet, the solution should change from yellow to blue at the equivalence point. However, the endpoint and the equivalence point are not necessarily equal. Ideally, the equivalence point is the endpoint. If the solution is overtitrated, the endpoint will be past the equivalence point.

Calculating the unknown concentration of a base from a titration

The unknown concentration of an acid or base may be determined by a titration. To determine the unknown concentration of a base, titrate a known volume of the base with an acid of known molarity. Use an acid–base indicator such as phenolphthalein to indicate when the titration has reached the equivalence point. If the solution is not overtitrated, the equivalence point will also be the endpoint. Then, calculate the concentration of the base using the formula $V_bN_b = V_aN_a$, where V_b represents the volume of the base, N_b represents the normality of the base, V_a represents the volume of the acid used in the titration, and N_a represents the normality of the acid used in the titration.

<u>Example</u>

> *During a titration, 20.0 mL of 0.0100 M NaOH is required to neutralize a 50.0 mL sample of HCl solution. Explain how to find the molarity of the HCl.*

To find the concentration of the unknown acid, use the formula $V_bN_b = V_aN_a$, where V_b represents the volume of the base, N_b represents the normality of the base, V_a represents the volume of the acid, and N_a represents the normality of the acid used in the titration. Solving the equation for the variable N_a yields $N_a = \frac{V_bN_b}{V_a}$. Because the molarity of the NaOH is 0.0100 M, the normality of the NAOH is 0.0100 N. Substituting in the appropriate values into the formula yields $N_a = \frac{(20.0 \text{ mL})(0.0100 \text{ N})}{50.0 \text{ mL}} = 0.00400$ N. Because HCl is monoprotic, the molarity of HCl is 0.00400 M.

Equilibrium Relationships in Acid-Base Chemistry

Strong/weak acids and bases

Acids or bases are categorized as strong or weak based on how completely they ionize in an aqueous solution. Strong acids and strong bases ionize essentially completely in an aqueous solution. Weak acids and weak bases ionize incompletely in an aqueous solution. Examples of strong acids include hydrochloric acid (HCl), sulfuric acid (H_2SO_4), and nitric acid (NO_3). Examples of weak acids are acetic acid ($HC_2H_3O_2$), hydrofluoric acid (HF), and carbonic acid (H_2CO_3). Examples of strong bases include sodium hydroxide (NaOH), potassium hydroxide (KOH), and calcium hydroxide (Ca(OH)$_2$). Ammonia (NH_3) is the most common weak base.

Monoprotic and polyprotic acids

Monoprotic acids are acids that have only one proton available to donate. Polyprotic acids have two or more protons available to donate. Typically, polyprotic acids donate their available protons in stages of one at a time. Specifically, diprotic acids can donate two protons, and triprotic acids can donate three protons. Common monoprotic acids include hydrochloric acid (HCl) and nitric acid (HNO_3). Common diprotic acids include sulfuric acid (H_2SO_4) and sulfurous acid (H_2SO_3). Phosphoric acid (H_3PO_4) is a common triprotic acid.

- 62 -

K_a of an acid and the K_b of a base

Given this general form for equilibrium of an acid in aqueous solution, HA (aq) + H_2O (l) $\leftrightarrow$ H_3O^+ (aq) + A^- (aq),the equilibrium constant expression is called the acid dissociation constant, K_a:

- $K_a = \frac{[H_3O^+][A^-]}{[HA]}$.

Strong acids have high K_a values because strong acids ionize essentially completely in aqueous solution. Weak acids have low K_a values because weak acids do not ionize completely in aqueous solution.

Given this general form for equilibrium of a base in aqueous solution, B (aq) + H_2O (l) $\leftrightarrow$ BH^+ (aq) + OH^- (aq),the equilibrium constant expression is called the base dissociation constant, K_b:

- $K_b = \frac{[BH^+][OH^-]}{[B]}$.

Strong bases have high K_b values because strong bases ionize essentially completely in aqueous solution. Weak bases have low K_b values because weak bases do not ionize completely in aqueous solution.

Hydrolysis

Hydrolysis is a chemical reaction between water and another reactant in which both compounds split apart. The water molecules split into hydrogen ions (H^+) and hydroxide ions (OH^-). The other compound splits into a cation and anion, too. Another way to state this is that hydrolysis is a decomposition reaction of a compound that is combined with water. The general form of a hydrolysis reaction is given by X^- (aq) + H_2O (l) $\leftrightarrow$ HX (aq) + OH^- (aq). A hydrolysis reaction is the reverse process of a neutralization reaction. A neutralization reaction is given by the general form: acid + base $\rightarrow$ salt + water. In general, a hydrolysis reaction may be thought of as salt + water $\rightarrow$ acid + base.

Buffer solution

A buffer solution is an aqueous solution that helps keep the pH highly constant. The addition of an acid or base to a buffer solution will not greatly affect the pH of that solution. A buffer consists of a weak acid and its conjugate base or a weak base and its conjugate acid. This combination of substances can remain in solution with each other without neutralizing each other. When acids or hydrogen ions (H^+) are added to a buffer solution, they are neutralized by the base in the buffer solution. When bases or hydroxide ions (OH^-) are added to a buffer solution, they are neutralized by the acid in the buffer solution.

Redox Processes

Oxidation-reduction reactions

An oxidation-reduction reaction is a reaction in which one of the reactants loses one or more electrons and the other reactant gains one or more electrons. The reactant that loses the electron(s) undergoes oxidation. The reactant that gains the electron(s) undergoes reduction. A common phrase to help remember this is *LEO the lion says GER*, where *LEO* represents *loss of electrons is oxidation* and *GER* represents *gain of electrons is reduction*. Oxidation cannot take place without reduction, and reduction cannot take place without oxidation.

Oxidation, reduction, oxidizing agent, reducing agent, oxidation states

Oxidation can be defined as any process involving a loss of one or more electrons.

Reduction can be defined as any process involving a gain of one or more electrons.

Oxidizing agent can be defined as the reactant in an oxidation-reduction reaction that causes oxidation. The oxidizing agent is reduced.

Reducing agent can be defined as the reactant in an oxidation-reduction reaction that causes reduction. The reducing agent is oxidized.

Oxidation states, also known as oxidation numbers, represent the charge that an atom has in a molecule or ion.

Oxidation state of an element in a molecule or ion

In order to determine the oxidation state of an element in a molecule or ion, apply these general rules: Hydrogen is usually assigned an oxidation state of +1 except for metal hydrides. Oxygen is usually assigned an oxidation state of −2 except for peroxides. Halogens are usually assigned oxidation states of −1 unless they are combined to a more electronegative element. Alkali metals are always assigned oxidation states of +1. Alkaline earth metals are always assigned oxidation states of +2. Finally, the sum of the oxidation states must equal the charge of the molecule or ion.

<u>Problems</u>

Determine the oxidation states for each element in each of the following:

1. H_2O
2. MgF_2
3. $Ca(NO_3)_2$

1. H_2O
Oxygen is usually assigned an oxidation state of –2, and hydrogen is usually assigned an oxidation state of +1. Check: $2(+1) + (-2) = 0$. Therefore, the oxidation states are as follows: hydrogen +1 and oxygen –2.

2. MgF_2
Halogens are usually assigned an oxidation state of –1, and alkaline earth metals are always assigned an oxidation state of +2. Check: $(+2) + 2(-1) = 0$. Therefore, the oxidation states are as follows: magnesium +2 and fluorine – 1.

3. $Ca(NO_3)_2$
Oxygen is usually assigned an oxidation number of –2, and alkaline earth metals are always assigned an oxidation state of +2. The oxidation state of nitrogen may be found by balancing the charges of the NO_3^-. Let x represent the charge of the nitrogen atom: $x + 3(-2) = -1$. Solving for x yields $x = +5$. Checking: $(+2) + 2[(+5) + 3(-2)] = 0$. Therefore, the oxidation states are as follows: calcium +2, nitrogen +5, and oxygen –2.

Determining if a reaction is an oxidation-reduction reaction

To determine if a reaction is an oxidation-reduction reaction, try to determine if one reactant is oxidized and the other reactant is reduced. First, assign oxidation states to each atom in the reaction. Remember that atoms of elements in their uncombined state are always assigned oxidation states of 0. Alkali metals are assigned +1, and alkaline earth metals are assigned +2. Oxygen is usually assigned –2, hydrogen is usually +1, and halogens are usually assigned –1. Write the half-reactions for each atom in the reactants, and determine if any are oxidized and reduced. If an oxidation reaction and a reduction reaction are present, the reaction is an oxidation-reduction reaction.

- 65 -

<u>Problems</u>

Determine whether each of the following reactions is an oxidation-reduction reaction.

1. $2Mg\,(s) + O_2\,(g) \rightarrow 2\,MgO\,(s)$.
2. $Ca\,(s) + 2HCl\,(aq) \rightarrow CaCl_2\,(aq) + H_2\,(g)$.

1. $2Mg(s) + O_2(g) \rightarrow 2MgO(s)$.

Assign oxidation states to each atom in the reaction. Atoms of an element in its uncombined state are always assigned 0. Therefore, both reactants are assigned 0. Oxygen is usually assigned –2, and magnesium is always assigned +2. Write the half-reactions:

- $Mg \rightarrow Mg^{2+} + 2e^-$ oxidation states of magnesium: $0 \rightarrow +2$.

- $O_2 + 2e^- \rightarrow O^{2-}$ oxidation states of oxygen: $0 \rightarrow -2$.

Magnesium is oxidized. Oxygen is reduced. Therefore, this is an oxidation-reduction reaction:

2. $Ca(s) + 2HCl\,(aq) \rightarrow CaCl_2\,(aq) + H_2\,(g)$.

The reactant $Ca\,(s)$ and the product $H_2\,(g)$ are assigned 0. Halogens such as chlorine are usually assigned –1. Hydrogen is usually assigned +1. Alkaline earth metals such as calcium are always assigned +2. Write the half-reactions:

- $Ca \rightarrow Ca^{2+} + 2e^-$ oxidation states of calcium: $0 \rightarrow +2$.

- $2Cl^- \rightarrow 2Cl^-$ oxidation states of chlorine: $-1 \rightarrow -1$.

- $2H^+ + 2e^- \rightarrow H_2$ oxidation states of hydrogen: $+1 \rightarrow 0$.

Calcium is oxidized. Hydrogen is reduced. Therefore, this is an oxidation-reduction reaction.

Organic Chemistry

Important Biochemical Compounds

Biochemical compounds

The four major classes of biochemical compounds are carbohydrates, lipids, proteins, and nucleic acids. Examples of carbohydrates include monosaccharides such as glucose, fructose, and ribose; disaccharides such as sucrose and lactose; and polysaccharides such as starch, cellulose, and glycogen. Examples of lipids include fatty acids, triglycerides, oils, lard, fat-soluble vitamins, waxes, and steroids such as cholesterol. Examples of proteins include enzymes, albumin, keratin, elastin, tubulin, collagen, hemoglobin, histones, and many hormones. Examples of nucleic acids include deoxyribonucleic acid (DNA) and ribonucleic acid (RNA).

Carbohydrates

Carbohydrates are organic compounds that produce energy. The empirical formula for most carbohydrates is CH_2O, which indicates that the ratio of carbon, hydrogen, and oxygen is always 1:2:1. The structure generally consists of aldehydes and ketones containing many hydroxyl groups. In general, carbohydrates are sugars and starches. Carbohydrates can be grouped as simple sugars or complex carbohydrates. The simple sugars include monosaccharides such as glucose and ribose and disaccharides such as sucrose and lactose. Complex carbohydrates are polymers of monosaccharides and include the polysaccharides such as cellulose, starch, and glycogen.

Monosaccharides, disaccharides, and polysaccharides

Monosaccharides, disaccharides, and polysaccharides are special types of organic compounds called carbohydrates, which are compounds composed of carbon, hydrogen, and oxygen. Monosaccharides and disaccharides are sugars. Monosaccharides are the simplest carbohydrates. Examples of monosaccharides are glucose, fructose (fruit sugar), ribose, and galactose. Disaccharides consist of two monosaccharides joined together. Examples of disaccharides include sucrose (table sugar), which is a compound of glucose and fructose, and lactose (milk sugar), which is a compound of glucose and galactose. Polysaccharides are polymers of monosaccharides. Examples of polysaccharides include cellulose, starch, and glycogen.

Lipids

Lipids have many functions. The main function of lipids is storing energy. One type of lipid is triglycerides, which include fats and oils. Lipids known as phospholipids also form the cell membranes of all plant and animal cells. Lipids can relay messages among cells in the nervous system and in the immune system. Some lipids are steroids, which serve many functions. For example, cholesterol helps make cell membranes pliable, and some steroids make up hormones such as testosterone and estrogen. Fat-soluble vitamins are also steroids.

Proteins

Proteins are polymers of amino acids. The amino acids are joined together by peptide bonds. The two major groups of proteins are fibrous proteins and globular proteins. Fibrous proteins provide structure in cells, bone tissue, connective tissue and line cartilage, tendons, and epidermal tissue. Examples of fibrous proteins include collage, elastin, and keratin. Globular proteins are huge folded molecules that include enzymes, hemoglobin, and some hormones. Antibodies are globular proteins that help defend the body from antigens. Some proteins such as actin and myosin are involved in muscle contraction. Some proteins act as storage containers for amino acids. Other proteins such as hemoglobin help transport materials throughout the body.

DNA and RNA

DNA, or deoxyribonucleic acid, is a two-stranded molecule in the shape of a double helix. DNA nucleotides consist of a deoxyribose (sugar), a phosphate, and a base. The bases are guanine, thymine, cytosine, and adenine. Guanine always pairs with cytosine, and thymine always pairs with adenine. If the double helix is compared to a twisted ladder, the legs of the ladder are the sugars and phosphates, and the rungs of the ladder consist of the bases. The bases that make up the rungs of the ladder are bound together with hydrogen bonds.

Deoxyribonucleic acid (DNA) and ribonucleic acid (RNA) are both nucleic acids composed of nucleotides, which have three of their four bases in common: guanine, adenine, and cytosine. The sugar in DNA nucleotides is deoxyribose, whereas the sugar in RNA nucleotides is ribose. DNA contains the base thymine, but RNA replaces thymine with uracil. DNA is double-stranded, and RNA is single-stranded. DNA has the shape of a double helix, whereas RNA is complexly folded. DNA stores the genetic information in the nucleus, while RNA has several forms. For example, mRNA, or messenger RNA, is a working copy of DNA, and tRNA, or transfer RNA, collects the needed amino acids for the ribosomes during the assembling of proteins.

Net equation for photosynthesis

Photosynthesis is the food-making process in green plants. Photosynthesis occurs in the chloroplasts of cells in the presence of light and chlorophyll. The reactants are carbon dioxide and water. The energy from the sunlight is absorbed and stored in the glucose molecules. The net equation for photosynthesis can be represented by the following equations:

- carbon dioxide + water + light $\xrightarrow{\text{chlorophyll}}$ glucose + oxygen
- $6CO_2 + 6H_2O + \text{light} \xrightarrow{\text{chlorophyll}} C_6H_{12}O_6 + 6O_2$.

The products of photosynthesis are glucose and oxygen gas. Glucose is a simple carbohydrate or sugar, which is a six-carbon monosaccharide.

Net equation for respiration

Cellular respiration is the process in which energy is released from glucose in the form of adenosine triphosphate (ATP). Cellular respiration is the reverse process of photosynthesis.

In cellular respiration, glucose is burned or combined with oxygen as shown in the following equations:

- glucose + oxygen → carbon dioxide + water + ATP
- $C_6H_{12}O_6 + 6O_2 \rightarrow 6CO_2 + 6H_2O$.

The products of cellular respiration are carbon dioxide and water. Energy is released from glucose in the form of ATP.

Common Organic Compounds

Organic compounds

Organic compounds are compounds that contain carbon. Carbon has only four valence electrons and will form four covalent bonds with hydrogen and other atoms or groups of atoms in order to satisfy the octet rule. Carbon can form single, double, and triple bonds with other atoms. Carbon can form long chains, branched chains, and rings in organic compounds. Hydrocarbons are organic compounds that contain only carbon and hydrogen. Substituted hydrocarbons are hydrocarbons that still have the carbon backbone, but one or more of the hydrogen atoms have been substituted with a different atom or group of atoms called a functional group. Functional groups may be single atoms such as in the halocarbons, in which a halogen such as chlorine or fluorine is substituted for a hydrogen atom. Some functional groups consist of more than one atom such as the alcohols, which have the hydroxyl (–OH) functional group.

Alcohol

An alcohol is a substituted hydrocarbon. The functional group of an alcohol is the hydroxyl (–OH). Examples of alcohols are methanol or methyl alcohol, CH_3OH (shown on the left), in which the hydroxyl group is substituted into methane; ethanol or ethyl alcohol, C_2H_5OH (shown in the middle), in which the hydroxyl is substituted into ethane; and isopropyl alcohol or 2-propanol C_3H_7OH (shown on the right), in which the hydroxyl group is substituted into the second carbon in propane.

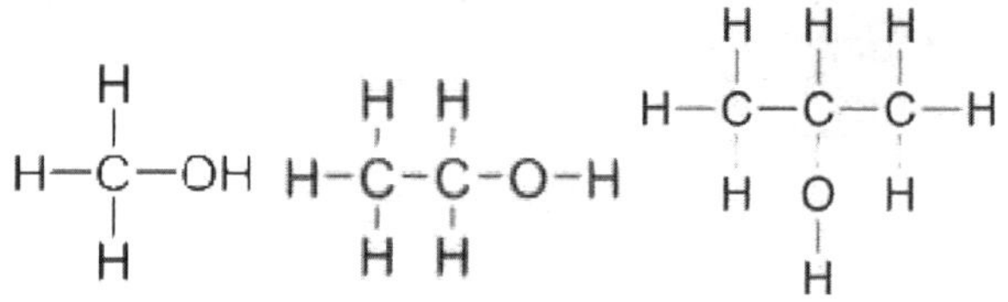

Alkanes, alkenes, and alkynes

Alkanes, alkenes, and alkynes are organic compounds called hydrocarbons, which consist only of carbon and hydrogen. Alkanes have only single bonds between their carbon atoms. Alkenes have at least one double bond between two of their carbon atoms. Alkynes have at least one triple bond between two of their carbon atoms. Alkanes are saturated hydrocarbons because they contain as many hydrogen atoms as possible due to their single bonds. Alkenes and alkynes are unsaturated hydrocarbons. Alkanes include methane (CH_4), ethane (C_2H_8), propane (C_3H_8), and butane (C_4H_{10}). Alkenes include ethene or ethylene

(C_2H_4), propene (C_3H_6), 1-butene (C_4H_8), and 1-pentene (C_5H_{10}). Alkynes include ethyne or acetylene (C_2H_2), 1-propyne (C_3H_4), 1-butyne (C_4H_6), and 1-pentyne (C_5H_8).

Aldehydes and ketones

An aldehyde is an organic compound with a functional group that consists of a carbon double bonded to an oxygen and single bonded to a hydrogen. This functional group is shown below on the left. For example, formaldehyde or methanal, CH_2O, is a methane molecule with this functional group substituted in for a hydrogen atom. Formaldehyde is shown below on the right.

A ketone is an organic compound with a functional group called a carbonyl (shown below on the left), which consists of a carbon double bonded to an oxygen atom and single bonded to two other carbon atoms. For example, acetone or propanone, C_3H_6O (shown below on the right), is a propane molecule with two of the hydrogen atoms on the second carbon atom replaced with one oxygen atom.

Ethers

Ethers are organic compounds containing an oxygen atom bonded to two alkyl or aryl groups. The general formula for an ether is R–O–R', where the oxygen is bonded to a carbon of the alkyl or aryl groups indicated by R and R'. For example, ethyl methyl ether or methoxyethane, C_3H_8O (shown on the left), has an ethyl group bonded to one side of an oxygen atom and a methyl group bonded to the other side of the oxygen. Diethyl ether or ethoxyethane (C_2H_5)$_2O$ (shown on the right), has an ethyl group bonded to each side of the oxygen atom.

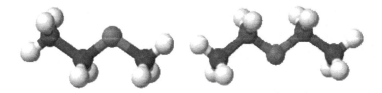

Measurement and Data Processing

Significant figures

Significant figures enable scientists to determine which measurements are very precise and which measurements are not as precise. Every measurement has uncertainty. When recording data, the use of the correct number of significant figures indicates the precision of the equipment being used to measure the data. In general, measurements are recorded only to the first uncertain digit. This means that the final recorded digit is considered to be uncertain. Every calculated value using collected data has uncertainty. Significant figures determine where to round when doing calculations with data. Also, significant figures prevent the answers to calculations from being stated with higher precision than the data used in the calculation would actually support.

When using significant figures in calculations, there are two sets of rules: one for addition and subtraction, and one for multiplication and division. For addition and subtraction calculations, answers should be rounded to the leftmost uncertain digit. For example, when adding measurements of 2.3 g and 10.81 g, the correct answer would be 13.1 g. The first term's uncertain digit is in the tenths place, while the second term's uncertain digit is in the hundredths place. Thus, the answer is rounded to the tenths place. In multiplication and division calculations, answers should be rounded to the exact number of significant figures in the factor that has the smallest number of significant figures. For example, when multiplying 3.2 by 4.001, the correct answer may only have 2 significant figures because 3.2 only has 2 significant figures. Therefore, the correct answer is 13. If the first factor were instead 3.20 or 3.200 (indicating that this value was known with greater precision), the answer would be 12.8 or 12.80, respectively.

Problems

Perform the following calculations using significant figures

1. 235.2008 + 304.02 + 467.9.
2. 1,303.69 – 1,245.
3. 400.0 × 2.3000.
4. 2.30/0.00040.

1. 235.2008 + 304.02 + 467.9.

When adding numbers using significant figures, the answer should be rounded to the place that has the greatest uncertainty. For these addends, the number 467.9 has the greatest uncertainty in the tenths place. Therefore, the correct answer is 1,007.1.

2. 1,303.69 – 1,245.

When subtracting numbers using significant figures, the answer should be rounded to the place that has the greatest uncertainty. In this problem, the number 1,245 has the greatest uncertainty in the ones place. Therefore, the correct answer is 59.

3. 400.0 × 2.3000.

When multiplying numbers using significant figures, determine the number of significant figures in each factor. The number 400.0 has four significant figures, and the number 2.3000 has five significant figures. Therefore, the answer should contain only four significant figures. The correct answer is 920.0.

4. 2.30/0.00040.

When dividing numbers using significant figures, determine the number of significant figures in each number involved in the calculation. The number 2.30 has three significant figures, and the number 0.00040 has two significant figures. Therefore, the answer should have only two significant figures. The correct answer is 5,800.

Proper organization and presentation of data

During a chemistry laboratory, all laboratory data should be collected in a lab notebook. All data should include the date and time collected. If possible, all data should be collected in structured tables. All appropriate raw data including units and uncertainties must be collected. The certain digits and the first uncertain or estimated digit should always be included. The raw data must be processed correctly. Calculations should be meticulous, keeping significant figures correct and units in order. Processed data should be presented in the form of graphs that highlight relationships, correlations, and trends. All graphs should have titles and be carefully labeled including the correct units. For example, scatterplots with lines of best fit could be used if the data show a linear relationship between variables.

Tables, graphs, and charts

When reading tables, graphs, and charts, determine if there is a correlation between the data for the independent variable and the data for the dependent variable. The correlation is positive if both data sets increase together. The correlation is negative if one set of data increases while the other set of data decreases. If a scatterplot is drawn, determine if there is a positive correlation, a negative correlation, or no correlation between the variables. If a correlation is found, determine if the correlation is linear or curvilinear. If there is a linear correlation, a line of best fit can be drawn to make predictions. Graphing calculators can be used to perform linear regression of the data and determine the equation for the line of best fit. Use of linear regression will increase the accuracy of predictions.

Converting from milligrams to kilograms and from kilograms to milligrams

One kilogram is equal to 1,000 g. One gram is equal to 1,000 mg. One way to convert between these units is the dimensional analysis method using the conversion factors of $\left(\frac{1\ kg}{1000\ g}\right)$ and $\left(\frac{1\ g}{1000\ mg}\right)$. For example, convert 5,400 mg to kg by multiplying (5,400

- 72 -

mg)$\left(\frac{1 \text{ g}}{1000 \text{ mg}}\right)\left(\frac{1 \text{kg}}{1000 \text{ g}}\right)$ = 5.4 × 10⁻³ kg. To convert 7,200 kg to mg, multiply (7,200

kg)$\left(\frac{1000 \text{ g}}{\text{kg}}\right)\left(\frac{1000 \text{ mg}}{\text{g}}\right)$ = 7.2 × 10⁹ mg.

Converting to and from degrees Fahrenheit, degrees Celsius, and kelvin

To convert from degrees Fahrenheit to degrees Celsius, use the formula $°C = \frac{5}{9}(°F - 32)$. To convert from degrees Celsius to degrees Fahrenheit, use the formula $°F = \frac{9}{5}°C + 32$. To convert from degrees Celsius to kelvin, use the formula K = °C + 273.15. To convert from kelvin to degrees Celsius, use the formula °C = K – 273.15. To convert from degrees Fahrenheit to kelvin, first convert the degrees Fahrenheit to degrees Celsius and then the degrees Celsius to kelvin. To convert from kelvin to degrees Fahrenheit, first convert the kelvin temperature to degrees Celsius and then convert the degrees Celsius to degrees Fahrenheit.

Metric units and symbols

Quantity	Name	Symbol
Mass	Kilogram	kg
Volume	Liter	L
Length	Meter	m
Time	Second	s
Absolute temperature	Kelvin	K
Amount of a substance	Mole	mole
Energy	Joule	J
Pressure	Pascal	Pa
Force	Newton	N
Frequency	Hertz	Hz
Electric current	Ampere	A
Luminous intensity	Candela	cd

Conversion problems

Perform each of the following conversions.

1. 250.0 mL to L
2. 0.050 mg to kg
3. 113 °F to K

1. 250.0 mL to L

Because 1 L contains 1,000 mL, the conversion factor is $\left(\frac{1 \text{ L}}{1,000 \text{ mL}}\right)$. Using dimensional analysis and multiplying, (250.0 mL)($\frac{1 \text{ L}}{1,000 \text{ mL}}$) = 0.2500 L.

2. 0.050 mg to kg

Because 1kg contains 1,000 g, and 1 g contains 1,000 mg, the conversion factors are $\left(\frac{1\ kg}{1{,}000\ g}\right)$ and $\left(\frac{1\ g}{1000\ mg}\right)$. Using dimensional analysis and multiplying, $(0.0500\ mg)\left(\frac{1\ g}{1{,}000\ mg}\right)\left(\frac{1\ kg}{1{,}000\ g}\right) = 5.00 \times 10^{-8}$ kg.

3. 113 °F to K

Substituting 113 °F into the formula °C = $\frac{5}{9}$(°F − 32) yields °C = $\frac{5}{9}$(113 − 32) = 45.0 °C. Then, substituting 45.0 °C into the formula K = °C + 273.15 yields K = 45.0 + 273.15 = 318 K.

Calculation problems

Perform the following calculations.

1. $(4.00 \times 10^{-3})(5.00 \times 10^{-2})$
2. $(8.0 \times 10^{4})/(4.0 \times 10^{-4})$

1. $(4.00 \times 10^{-3})(5.00 \times 10^{-2})$

To multiply numbers that are written in scientific notation, first multiply the coefficients. In this problem, (4.00)(5.00) = 20.0. Next, add the exponents. In this problem, (−3) + (−2) = −5. If the new coefficient had been less than 10, the calculation would be done. However, in this problem, combining the coefficient with the new base yields 20.0×10^{-5}, which is not written in correct scientific notation. When this occurs, move the decimal to the left until the coefficient is between 1 and 10 and then adjust the exponent accordingly. In this problem, the correct answer is 2.0×10^{-4}.

2. $(8.0 \times 10^{4})/(4.0 \times 10^{-4})$

To divide numbers that are written in scientific notation, divide the coefficients and subtract the exponents. In this problem, 8.0/4.0 = 2.0, and 4 − (−4) = 8. The correct answer is 2.0×10^{8}.

Scientific notation

Scientific notation is a convenient way to write extremely large or extremely small numbers. Any rational number can be written in scientific notation. The format is $M \times 10^{n}$, where M is a number between 1 and 10 and n is a positive or negative integer. The first number (M) is called the coefficient, and the second number (10^{n}) is called the base. For numbers greater than 1, n is positive. For numbers less than 1, n is negative. For example, the number 6,200,000 is written as 6.2×10^{6}, and the number 0.000047 is written as 4.7×10^{-5}. To convert from scientific notation, simply move the decimal point the same number of places as the exponent. Move the decimal to the right if the exponent is positive and to the left if the exponent is negative. For example, 3.1×10^{4} is 31,000, and 8.6×10^{-3} is 0.0086.

Basic measurement equipment

Chemistry laboratories should be equipped with the following basic measurement equipment: triple-beam balances or digital balances for measuring mass, graduated cylinders for measuring volumes of liquids, graduated pipettes for measuring small volumes of liquids, thermometers for measuring temperature, pH meters for measuring pH, and rulers for measuring length. Manometers may also be used to measure the pressure of gases. Burettes may be used to measure volumes of acids or bases used in titrations. Viscometers may be used to determine the viscosity of liquids.

<u>Problem</u>

> *Calculate the mean of the following data: 2.300, 2.410, 2.210, 2.350, 2.300, 2.210.*

> The mean is the average of a group of data. To find the mean, find the sum of the data and then divide the sum by the number of data points. For example, to find the average of the data: 2.300, 2.410, 2.210, 2.350, 2.300, 2.210, first, find the sum of $2.300 + 2.410 + 2.210 + 2.350 + 2.300 + 2.210 = 13.78$. Next, divide the sum of 13.78 by 6 because there are six data points. This yields $13.78/6 = 2.297$.

Accuracy and precision

Accuracy is the exactness of a measurement or how close a measurement is to the actual value. Precision is the consistency of a measurement or the repeatability of a measurement. For example, the figure on the left represents dart throwing that is neither precise nor accurate because there is no grouping of the darts nor are any darts close to the bull's-eye. The figure in the middle represents dart throwing that is precise due to the grouping of the darts but not accurate due to the location of the group. The figure on the right represents dart throwing that is precise and accurate due to the grouping of the darts and the location of the grouping near the bull's-eye.

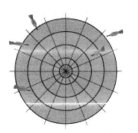   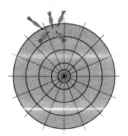   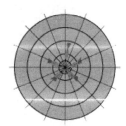

neither precise   precise, but   precise and
nor accurate   not accurate   accurate

<u>Example</u>

Given these data from two balances in a chemistry laboratory, explain how to determine which of the two balances is more accurate and more precise if the actual mass of the sample is 7.823 g.

Trial	Triple-Beam Balance	Digital Balance
1	7.81 g	7.824 g
2	7.82 g	7.823 g
3	7.79 g	7.824 g
4	7.80 g	7.823 g
5	7.81 g	7.824 g

In order to determine which balance is more accurate, find the range of differences of each measured value and the actual value for each balance. The range of differences for the triple-beam balance is between 0.003 and 0.023. The range of differences for the digital balance is between 0.000 and 0.001. Therefore, the digital balance is more accurate. In order to determine which balance is more precise, find the difference between the highest and lowest readings for each balance. The range of the data for the triple beam balance is 0.02. The range of the data for the digital balance is 0.001. Therefore, the digital balance is also more precise.

Random error, systematic error, and personal error

Random error is also known as indeterminate error. Random errors are from unknown causes and are unpredictable. Systematic error is also known as determinate error. Systematic error is introduced into the data due to some defect in a procedure or an instrument that is faulty or not properly calibrated. For example, measurements that have errors due to imprecise tools are systematic errors. Systematic errors are difficult to detect and eliminate. Personal error is introduced into the data due to human mistakes. This would include the improper use of equipment, improperly following a procedure, and the incorrect reading of data. Personal error can often be minimized with proper training. Random error can cause random fluctuations in the data that are above or below the actual values. Systematic error will cause the data to be consistently high or consistently low. For example, a balance that is calibrated low by 0.01 g or a thermometer that is calibrated 3 °C low will each consistently provide low readings.

Percent error

Percent error expresses the difference between the experimental value and the theoretical value (or actual value) and is written as a percent. To calculate percent error, subtract the theoretical value from the experimental value and divide the difference by the theoretical value. Then, multiply by 100 to convert this decimal to a percent. Finally, add a percent sign. If the situation is not appropriate to use a negative percent, then take the absolute value of the numerator before dividing:

$$\text{percent error} = \frac{\text{experimental value} - \text{theoretical value}}{\text{theoretical value}} \times 100\ \%.$$

Example

In a laboratory experiment, the specific heat of a sample of copper is calculated to be 0.40 J/(g·°C). The actual specific heat of copper is 0.38 J/(g·°C). Explain how to calculate the percent error.

The percent error in the specific heat calculation can be calculated using the following formula:

- percent error $= \dfrac{\text{experimental value} - \text{theoretical value}}{\text{theoretical value}} \times 100 \text{ \%.}$

Substituting in 0.40 J/(g·°C) for the experimental value and 0.38 J/(g·°C) in for the theoretical value yields the following:

percent error $= \dfrac{0.40 \text{ J/(g·°C)} - 0.38 \text{ J/(g·°C)}}{0.38 \text{ J/(g·°C)}} \times 100 \text{ \%} = 5.3 \text{ \%}$. Note that the theoretical value is in the denominator. Also, after performing the division, the answer is in decimal form. Multiply by 100 to change the decimal to a percent, and then add the percent symbol.

Practice Test

Multiple Choice Questions

1. Which substance is most likely to be a solid at STP?
   a. Kr
   b. Na
   c. NH_3
   d. Xe

2. Which of the following tend to increase the melting point of a solid?
   I. Increasing molecular weight
   II. Decreasing polarity
   III. Increasing surface area
   a. I and II
   b. II
   c. III
   d. I and III

3. A gas at constant volume is cooled. Which statement about the gas must be true?
   a. The kinetic energy of the gas molecules has decreased.
   b. The gas has condensed to a liquid.
   c. The weight of the gas has decreased.
   d. The density of the gas has increased.

4. A weather balloon is filled with 1000 mol of He gas at 25 °C and 101 kPa of pressure. What is the volume of the weather balloon?
   a. 24518 m3
   b. 24.5 m3
   c. 2 m3
   d. 245 m^3

5. One mole of oxygen gas and two moles of hydrogen are combined in a sealed container at STP. Which of the following statements is true?
   a. The mass of hydrogen gas is greater than the mass of oxygen.
   b. The volume of hydrogen is greater than the volume of oxygen.
   c. The hydrogen and oxygen will react to produce 2 mol of water.
   d. The partial pressure of hydrogen is greater than the partial pressure of oxygen.

6. Graham's law is best used to determine what relationship between two different materials?
   a. pressure and volume
   b. volume and temperature
   c. mass and diffusion rate
   d. Diffusion rate and temperature

7. Which is the correct order of increasing intermolecular attractive forces?
   a. Dipole-dipole<ionic<hydrogen bonding<London dispersion
   b. Ionic<dipole-dipole<London dispersion<hydrogen bonding
   c. Hydrogen bonding<London dispersion<ionic<dipole-dipole
   d. London dispersion<dipole-dipole<hydrogen bonding<ionic

8. One mole of an ideal gas is compressed to 10 L and heated to 25 °C. What is the pressure of the gas?
   a. 2.4 KPa
   b. 2.4 atm
   c. 0.2 atm
   d. 0.2 KPa

9. A 10 L cylinder contains 4 moles of oxygen, 3 moles of nitrogen and 7 moles of neon. The temperature of the cylinder is increased from 20 °C to 40 °C. Determine the partial pressure of neon in the cylinder as a percentage of the whole.
   a. 50%
   b. 70%
   c. 90%
   d. 40%

10. Three liquids, X, Y and Z are placed in separate flasks, each of which is suspended in a water bath at 75 °C. The boiling points of each liquid are
   X, 273 K
   Y, 340 K
   Z, 360 K
Which of the three liquids will begin to boil after warming to 75 °C?
   a. X, Y, and Z
   b. X and Z
   c. X and Y
   d. Y and Z

11. Which of the following statements is true about the physical properties of liquids and gases?
   I. Liquids and gases are both compressible
   II. Liquids flow, but gases do not
   III. Liquids flow and gases are incompressible
   IV. Liquids flow and gases are compressible
   V. Gases flow and liquids are incompressible
   a. I and III
   b. II and IV
   c. III and V
   d. IV and V

12. Which of the following statements **generally** describes the trend of electronegativity considering the Periodic Table of the Elements?
   a. Electronegativity increases going from left to right and from top to bottom
   b. Electronegativity increases going from right to left and from bottom to top
   c. Electronegativity increases going from left to right and from bottom to top
   d. Electronegativity increases going from right to left and from top to bottom

13. Gas X is in a cylinder at 1 atm of pressure and has a volume of 10 L at 0° C. Gas X spontaneously decomposes to gas Y, according to the equation

$$X \longrightarrow 3Y$$

The temperature in the cylinder remains the same during the reaction. What is the pressure in the cylinder now?
   a. 1 atm
   b. 3 atm
   c. 4 atm
   d. Cannot be determined

14. 1 mole of water and 1 mole of argon are in a cylinder at 110 °C and 1 atm of pressure. The temperature of the cylinder is reduced to -5 °C. Which statement about the contents of the cylinder is most accurate?
   a. The pressure in the cylinder is decreased, and the partial pressure of argon is less than that of water.
   b. The pressure in the cylinder is about the same, and the partial pressure of water is less than that of argon.
   c. The pressure in the cylinder is decreased, and the partial pressure of water is much less than that of argon.
   d. The pressure in the cylinder is decreased and the partial pressure of water is the same as argon.

15. A solid is heated until it melts. Which of the following is true about the solid melting?
   a. ΔH is positive, and ΔS is positive
   b. ΔH is negative and ΔS is positive
   c. ΔH is positive and ΔS is negative
   d. ΔH is negative and ΔS is negative

16. A liquid is held at its freezing point and slowly allowed to solidify. Which of the following statements about this event are true?
   a. During freezing, the temperature of the material decreases
   b. While freezing, heat is given off by the material
   c. During freezing, heat is absorbed by the material
   d. During freezing, the temperature of the material increases

17. A liquid is heated from 50 °C to 80 °C. Which of the following statements is generally true about the solubility of solids and gases in the liquid?
   a. The solubility of solids will increase and the solubility of gases will decrease
   b. The solubility of solids will decrease and the solubility of gases will increase
   c. The solubility of solids will increase and the solubility of gases will increase
   d. The solubility of solids will decrease and the solubility of gases will decrease

18. 100 g of H_3PO_4 is dissolved in water, producing 400 mL of solution. What is the normality of the solution?
   a. 2.55 N
   b. 1.02 N
   c. 7.65 N
   d. 0.25 N

19. Silver nitrate ($AgNO_3$) is dissolved in water. One drop of an aqueous solution containing NaCl is added and almost instantly, a white milky precipitate forms. What is the precipitate?
    a. NaCl
    b. $NaNO_3$
    c. $AgNO_3$
    d. AgCl

20. 100 g of ethanol C_2H_6O is dissolved in 100 g of water. The final solution has a volume of 0.2 L. What is the density of the resulting solution?
    a. 0.5 g/mL
    b. 1 g/mL
    c. 46 g/mL
    d. 40 g/mL

21. 100 mL of a 0.1 M solution of NaOH is neutralized to pH 7 with H_2SO_4. How many grams of H_2SO_4 are required to achieve this neutralization?
    a. 4.9 g
    b. 0.98 g
    c. 9.8 g
    d. 0.49 g

22. Comparing pure water and a 1 M aqueous solution of NaCl, both at 1 atm of pressure, which of the following statements is most accurate?
    a. The pure water will boil at a higher temperature, and be less conductive
    b. The pure water will boil at a lower temperature and be less conductive
    c. The pure water will boil at a lower temperature and be more conductive
    d. The pure water boil at the same temperature and be more conductive

23. Place the following in the correct order of increasing acidity.
    a. HCl<HF<HI<HBr
    b. HCl<HBr<HI<HF
    c. HI<HBr<HCl<HF
    d. HF<HCl<HBr<HI

24. Place the following in the correct order of increasing solubility in water.
    a. Butanol<ethanol<octane<NaCl
    b. Ethanol<NaCl<octane<butanol
    c. NaCl<octane<butanol<ethanol
    d. Octane<butanol<ethanol<NaCl

25. 50 grams of acetic acid $C_2H_4O_2$ are dissolved in 200 g of water. Calculate the weight % and mole fraction of the acetic acid in the solution.
    a. 20%, 0.069
    b. 0.069%, 0.20
    c. 25%, 0.075
    d. 20%, 0.075

26. Ammonium Phosphate $(NH_4)_3PO_4$ is a strong electrolyte. What will be the concentration of all the ions in a 0.9 M solution of ammonium phosphate?
   a. 0.9 M NH_4^+, 0.9 M PO_4^{3-}
   b. 0.3 M NH_4^+, 0.9 M PO_4^{3-}
   c. 2.7 M NH_4^+, 0.9 M PO_4^{3-}
   d. 2.7 M NH_4^+, 2.7 M PO_4^{3-}

27. Which of the following represents the correct increasing order of acidity?
   a. $CH_3COOH < CH_3OH < CH_3CH_3 < HCl$
   b. $CH_3CH_3 < CH_3OH < CH_3COOH < HCl$
   c. $CH_3CH_3 < CH_3COOH < CH_3OH < HCl$
   d. $CH_3OH < CH_3CH_3 < HCl < CH_3COOH$

28. One liter of a 0.02 M solution of methanol in water is prepared. What is the mass of methanol in the solution, and what is the approximate molality of methanol?
   a. 0.64 g, 0.02 m
   b. 0.32 g, 0.01 m
   c. 0.64 g, 0.03 m
   d. 0.32 g, 0.02 m

29. A 1 M solution of NaCl (A) and a 0.5 M solution of NaCl (B) are joined together by a semi permeable membrane. What, if anything, is likely to happen between the two solutions?
   a. No change, the solvents and solutes are the same in each
   b. Water will migrate from A to B
   c. NaCl will migrate from A to B and water will migrate from B to A.
   d. Water will migrate from B to A.

30. Which of the following radioactive emissions results in an increase in atomic number?
   a. Alpha
   b. Negative Beta
   c. Positive Beta
   d. Gamma

31. A material has a half life of 2 years. If you started with 1 kg of the material, how much would be left after 8 years?
   a. 1 kg
   b. 0.5 kg
   c. 0.06 kg
   d. 0.12 kg

32. C-14 has a half life of 5730 years. If you started with 1 mg of C-14 today, how much would be left in 20,000 years?
   a. 0.06 mg
   b. 0.07 mg
   c. 0.11 mg
   d. 0.09 mg

33. The best way to separate isotopes of the same element is to exploit:
    a. Differences in chemical reactivity
    b. Differences in reduction potential
    c. Differences in toxicity
    d. Differences in mass

34. Nuclear chain reactions, such as the one that is exploited in nuclear power plants, are propagated by what subatomic particle(s)?
    a. Protons
    b. Neutrons
    c. Electrons
    d. Neutrons and protons

35. Which of the following statements about radioactive decay is true?
    a. The sum of the mass of the daughter particles is less than that of the parent nucleus
    b. The sum of the mass of the daughter particles is greater than that of the parent nucleus
    c. The sum of the mass of the daughter particles is equal to that of the parent nucleus
    d. The sum of the mass of the daughter particles cannot be accurately measured

36. Determine the number of neutrons, protons and electrons in ^{238}U.
    a. 238, 92, 238
    b. 92, 146, 146
    c. 146, 92, 92
    d. 92, 92, 146

37. An alpha particle consists of
    a. Two electrons and two protons
    b. Two electrons and two neutrons
    c. Four neutrons
    d. Two protons and two neutrons

38. Describe the correct outer shell electronic arrangement of phosphorous.
    a. $4s^2 \, 4p^3$
    b. $3s^2 \, 3p^3$
    c. $2s^2 \, 3p^3$
    d. $2s^2 \, 2p^3$

39. Hund's rule regarding electronic configuration states:
    a. Electrons in the same orbital must have an opposite spin
    b. Electrons must fill lower energy orbitals before filling higher energy orbitals
    c. Electrons must populate empty orbitals of equal energy before filling occupied orbitals
    d. Electrons must have the same nuclear spin as the nucleus

40. Arrange the following elements in order of increasing atomic radius:
    a. K<Zn<Fe<As<Kr
    b. K<Fe<Zn<Kr<As
    c. Kr<As<Fe<K<Zn
    d. Kr<As<Zn<Fe<K

41. When a solid is heated and transforms directly to the gaseous phases, this process is called:
   a. sublimation
   b. fusion
   c. diffusion
   d. condensation

42. Determine the oxidation states of each of the elements in $KMnO_4$:
   a. K^{+1}, Mn^{+7}, O^{-8}
   b. K^{-1}, Mn^{+7}, O^{-2}
   c. K^{+1}, Mn^{+3}, O^{-4}
   d. K^{+1}, Mn^{+7}, O^{-2}

43. Place the following elements in order of decreasing electronegativity:
      N, As, Bi, P, Sb
   a. As>Bi>N>P>Sb
   b. N>P>As>Sb>Bi
   c. Bi>Sb>As>P>N
   d. P>N>As>Sb>Bi

44. Arrange the following compounds from most polar to least polar:
      F_2, CH_3CH_2Cl, NaCl, CH_3OH
   a. NaCl>CH_3OH> CH_3CH_2Cl> F_2
   b. F_2> NaCl> CH_3OH>CH_3CH_2Cl
   c. CH_3OH>NaCl>F_2>CH_3CH_2Cl
   d. NaCl>F_2>CH_3OH>CH_3CH_2Cl

45. Which of the following is an incorrect Lewis structure?

I. 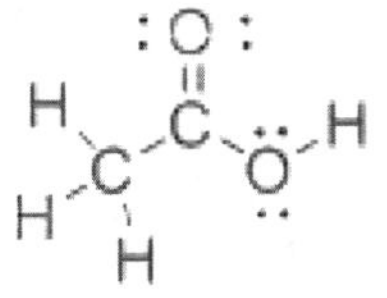 [structure]   II. 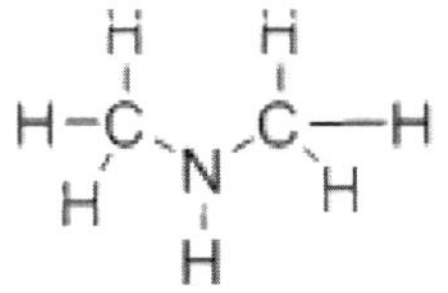 [structure]   III. 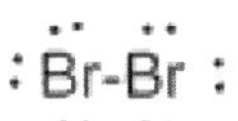 :Br-Br: IV. 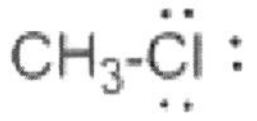 CH_3-Cl:

   a. I
   b. II
   c. III
   d. IV

46. Which bond has the shortest length?
   a. sp^2
   b. sp^3
   c. sp
   d. pi

- 84 -

47. Resonance structures can be defined as:
    a. Two or more structures that have different atoms bound to different atoms
    b. Two structures that have a similar structure but different formula
    c. Two or more structures that have the same formula, but are different in shape
    d. Two or more structures that differ only in the arrangement of electrons in the structures

48. Atoms that are sp^2 hybridized will have what sort of hybrid orbital geometry around them?
    a. Tetrahedral
    b. Trigonal planar
    c. Linear
    d. Angled

49. What is the chemical composition of ammonium sulfate?
    a. N 21%, H 3%, S 24%, O 32%
    b. N 10%, H 6%, S 24%, O 60%
    c. N 10%, H 4%, S 12%, O 74%
    d. N 21%, H 6%, S 24%, O 48%

50. What is the correct IUPAC name of the compound Fe_2O_3?
    a. Iron (I) oxide
    b. Iron (II) oxide
    c. Iron (III) oxide
    d. Iron (IV) oxide

51. Balance the following reaction between sulfuric acid and aluminum hydroxide by filling in the correct stoichiometric values for each chemical.
    $$\_\ H_2SO_4 + \_\ Al(OH)_3 \rightarrow \_\ Al_2(SO_4)_3 + \_\ H_2O$$
    a. 3, 2, 1, 6
    b. 2, 3, 1, 3
    c. 3, 3, 2, 6
    d. 1, 2, 1, 4

52. Calculate the mass of water produced from the reaction of 1 kg of n-heptane with oxygen.
    $$n\text{-}heptane\ (1\ kg) + 11\ O_2 \rightarrow 7\ CO_2 + 8\ H_2O$$
    a. 144 g
    b. 8 kg
    c. 800 g
    d. 1.4 kg

53. Magnesium metal is reacted with hydrobromic acid according to the following equation:
    $$Mg + 2HBr \rightarrow MgBr_2 + H_2$$
    If 100 g of Mg is reacted with 100 g of HBr, which statement about the reaction is true?
    a. Mg is the limiting reagent
    b. HBr is the excess reagent
    c. Mg is the excess reagent
    d. 100 g of $MgBr_2$ will be produced

54. Methane gas is burned in pure oxygen at 200 °C and 1 atm of pressure to produce CO_2 and H_2O according to the equation

$$CH_4 + 2O_2 \rightarrow CO_2 + 2H_2O$$

If 10 L of methane gas were burned, and the final temperature and pressure remained the same, how many liters of gaseous products are produced by the reaction?

    a. 10 L
    b. 20 L
    c. 30 L
    d. 40 L

55. The overall reaction A→D can be described by the following equation:

$$A \xrightarrow{\text{fast}} B \xrightarrow{\text{slow}} C \xrightarrow{\text{fast}} D$$

What would be the rate law for the overall reaction of A to D?

    a. Rate = k[D]/[A]
    b. Rate = k[B]
    c. Rate = [B]
    d. Rate = k[C]/[B]

56. How many electrons are in an uncharged atom of $^{45}_{20}Ca$?

    a. 20
    b. 45
    c. 65
    d. 25

57. For the reaction $CO_2(g) + H_2(g) \rightarrow CO(g) + H_2O(l)$, which of the following will occur if the pressure of the reaction is increased?

    a. The reaction rate will increase
    b. The reaction rate will decrease
    c. The reaction equilibrium will shift to the right
    d. The reaction equilibrium will shift to the left

58. For the gas phase reaction $CH_4 + 4Cl_2 \rightarrow CCl_4 + 4HCl$, what would be the equilibrium expression K_{eq} for this reaction?

    a. $[CH_4][Cl_2] / [CCl_4][4HCl]$
    b. $[CH_4][Cl_2] / [CCl_4][HCl]^4$
    c. $[4Cl][CCl_4\}/[CH_4][4HCl]$
    d. $[CCl_4][HCl]^4/ [CH_4][Cl_2]^4$

59. Adding a catalyst to a reaction will do which of the following to that reaction:

    a. Shift the reaction equilibrium towards the products
    b. Increase the temperature of the reaction
    c. Decrease the energy of activation for the reaction
    d. Increase the purity of the reaction products

60. 10 g of salt XY (MW = 100 g/mol) is added to 1 liter of water with stirring. The salt dissociates into ions X^+ and Y^-. After equilibrium is established, the undissolved portion of the salt was removed by filtration, weighed, and found to be 9.5 g. What is the K_{sp} for this salt?

  a. 5×10^{-2}
  b. 5×10^{-3}
  c. 1×10^{-2}
  d. 2.5×10^{-5}

61. Which of the following are considered Lewis acids?

  I. H_2SO_4
  II. $AlCl_3$
  III. PCl_3
  IV. $FeCl_3$
  a. II and IV
  b. II and III
  c. I and IV
  d. I and II

62. Place the following in the correct order of increasing acidity:

  H_3PO_4, HF, HCl, H_2O, NH_3
  a. $H_3PO4 < H_2O < NH_3 < HF < HCl$
  b. $NH_3 < H_2O < HF < H_3PO_4 < HCl$
  c. $H_2O < NH_3 < HF < H_3PO_4 < HCl$
  d. $NH_3 < H_2O < HF < HCl < H_3PO_4$

63. The pka for ethanol (CH_3CH_2OH) is approximately 16. The pka for acetic acid (CH_3COOH) is about 4. The difference can be explained by:

  a. Resonance stabilization
  b. Electronegativity differences
  c. Molecular weight differences
  d. Molecular size differences

64. What will be the pH of 2 L of a 0.1 M aqueous solution of HCl?

  a. 2
  b. -1
  c. 1
  d. 0.05

65. What is the pH of a buffer containing 0.2 M NaOAc and 0.1 M AcOH? The pka of acetic acid is 4.75.

  a. 4
  b. 5
  c. 6
  d. 7

66. 50 mL of 1 M H_2SO_4 is added to an aqueous solution containing 4 g of NaOH. What will the final pH of the resulting solution be?

    a. 5

    b. 6

    c. 7

    d. 9

67. To make a good buffering system in the pH range of 5-9, which acid/base combinations would likely work the best?

    a. HCl/NaOH

    b. $HNO_3/NaNO_3$

    c. $H_2SO_4/NaHSO_4$

    d. NaH_2PO_4/Na_2HPO_4

68. For the conversion of water into steam, which of the following is true?

    a. $\Delta T=0$, $\Delta S>0$

    b. $\Delta T>0$, $\Delta S = 0$

    c. $\Delta T =0$, $\Delta S <0$

    d. $\Delta T >0$, $\Delta S >0$

69. 100 g of NH_3 are cooled from 100 °C to 25 °C. What is the heat change for this transition? The heat capacity of ammonia gas is 35.1 J/(mol) (°K)

    a. -263KJ

    b. 15.5 KJ

    c. -15.5KJ

    d. 263 KJ

70. Determine the heat of combustion for the following reaction:

    Propane + 5 O_2 →3 CO_2 + 4 H_2O

The standard heats of formation for propane, CO_2 and water are -103.8 KJ/mol, -393.5 KJ/mol and -285.8 KJ/mol respectively.

    a. -2220 KJ/mol

    b. -2323.7 kJ/mol

    c. 2220 KJ/mol

    d. 2323.7 KJ/mol

71. Which of the following reactions produces products with higher entropy than the starting materials?

    I. Glucose (s) + water →glucose (aq)

    II. 4Al (s) + 3O_2(g)→2Al_2O_3(s)

    III. Br_2 + light→2 Br

    IV. Ice →water vapor

    a. II, III

    b. I, II

    c. I, III

    d. I, III, IV

72. A 1kg block each of iron, lead and nickel are heated from 20 °C to 30 °C. Which of the following statements about the blocks is true?
   a. The lead will heat faster than the iron and the nickel.
   b. The iron required more heat to reach 30 °C than the nickel or lead.
   c. All three blocks required a different amount of heat to reach 30 °C.
   d. The iron required more time to reach 30 °C.

73. In the reaction $Pb + H_2SO_4 + H_2O \rightarrow PbSO_4 + H_2 + H_2O$
   a. Lead is reduced and hydrogen is oxidized
   b. Lead is oxidized and hydrogen is oxidized
   c. Lead is reduced and sulfate is oxidized
   d. Lead is oxidized and hydrogen is reduced

74. Which of the following elements would likely be good reducing agents?
   a. Br_2
   b. N_2
   c. Na
   d. Ne

75. Molten magnesium chloride is electrolyzed. The products formed from this reaction are:
   a. Mg(0) at the anode and Cl- at the cathode
   b. Mg2+ at the anode and Cl- at the cathode
   c. Mg (0) at the cathode and Cl_2 at the anode
   d. Mg(0) at the anode and Cl_2 at the cathode

76. The transformation of diamond to graphite has a $-\Delta G$. Which of the following is true?
   a. The reaction is spontaneous and occurs rapidly at room temperature
   b. The reaction is not spontaneous and occurs slowly at room temperature
   c. The reaction is not spontaneous and does not occur at room temperature
   d. The reaction is spontaneous and occurs slowly at room temperature

77. What would be the correct IUPAC name for the following compound?

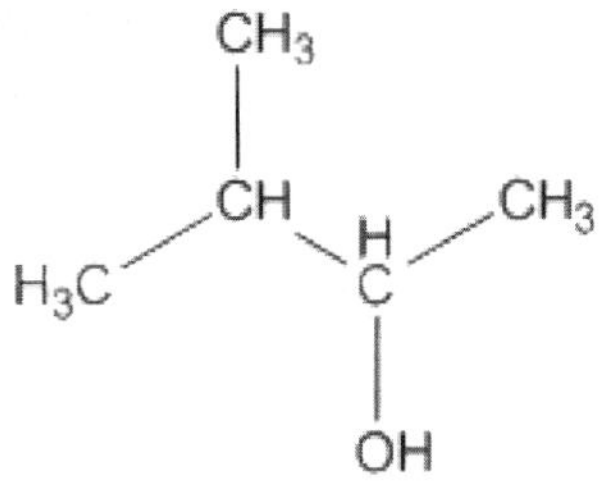

   a. 3-methyl-2-butanol
   b. 2-methyl-3-butanol
   c. 3,3-dimethyl-2-propanol
   d. 2-Hydroxy-3-methyl butane

78. Which of the following molecules is an alkene?

I.    II.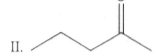

III. 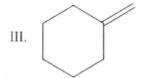   IV.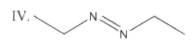

   a. I
   b. II
   c. III
   d. IV

79. What is the oxidation state of the carbon atom in a carboxylic acid functional group?
   a. 4+
   b. 3+
   c. 2-
   d. 3-

80. Which of the following molecules is named correctly?

A.

methyl propionoate

B.   OH

1-propanol

C.

3-propanoic acid

D.

3-butene

81. Which scientist was responsible for developing the format of the modern periodic table?
   a. Faraday
   b. Einstein
   c. Hess
   d. Mendeleev

82. Two different molecules can be isomers of each other if:
    a. They have the same functional groups
    b. They have the same oxidation state
    c. They have the same molecular weight
    d. They have the same chemical formula

83. Which of the following molecules are cis alkenes?

I.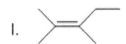

II.

III.

IV.

    a. I, II
    b. II, III
    c. III, IV
    d. I, IV

84. What would be the best analytical tool for determining the chemical structure of an organic compound?
    a. NMR
    b. HPLC
    c. IR
    d. Mass spec

85. Proteins are made up of which of the following repeating subunits?
    a. Sugars
    b. Triglycerides
    c. Amino acids
    d. Nucleic acids

86. The precision of a number of data points refers to:
    a. How accurate the data is
    b. How many errors the data contains
    c. How close the data points are to the mean of the data
    d. How close the actual data is to the predicted result

87. The density of a material refers to:
    a. Mass per volume
    b. Mass per mole
    c. Molecular weight per volume
    d. Moles per volume

88. Which of the following types of chemicals are considered generally unsafe to store together?

    I. Liquids and solids
    II. Acids and bases
    III. Reducing agents and oxidizing agents
    IV. Metals and salts

  a. I, II
  b. II, III
  c. III, IV
  d. I, IV

89. Which statement about the impact of chemistry on society is not true?
  a. Fluoridation of water has had no effect on the rate of cavities as compared to unfluoridated water
  b. Chemical fertilizers have tremendously increased food production per acre in the U.S.
  c. Chemistry played a central role in the development of nuclear weapons
  d. Use of catalytic converters in automobiles has greatly reduced acid rain producing exhaust products

90. Methyl mercury is a toxin produced indirectly from what energy source?
  a. Oil
  b. Natural gas
  c. Wood
  d. Coal

Multiple Choice Answers

1. B: Na (sodium) is a solid at standard temperature and pressure, which is 0°C (273 K) and 100 kPa (0.986 atm), according to IUPAC. The stronger the intermolecular forces, the greater the likelihood of the material being a solid. Kr and Xe are noble gases and have negligible intermolecular attraction. NH_3 has some hydrogen bonding but is still a gas at STP. Sodium is an alkali metal whose atoms are bonded by metallic bonding and is therefore a solid at STP.

2. D: Generally, the larger and heavier the molecule, the higher the melting point. Decreasing polarity will lower intermolecular attractions and lower the melting point. Long, linear molecules have a larger surface area, and therefore more opportunity to interact with other molecules, which increases the melting point.

3. A: The kinetic energy of the gas molecules is directly proportional to the temperature. If the temperature decreases, so does the molecular motion. A decrease in temperature will not necessarily mean a gas condenses to a liquid. Neither the mass nor the density is impacted, as no material was added or removed, and the volume remained the same.

4. B: The ideal gas law PV=nRT is rearranged to solve for V, and we get V = nRT/P. R is the gas constant, 0.08206 L atm/mol K, and the Celsius temperature must be converted to Kelvin, by adding 273 to 25°C to obtain 298 K. The pressure must be converted to atmospheres, which 101 kPa is essentially 1 atm (0.9967 atm). Plugging the numbers into the equation we get V = 1000 mol (0.08206 L atm/mol K)(298 K)/1 atm, which gives V = 24,453 L. A liter is a cubic decimeter (dm^3) and when converted gives V = 24.5 m^3.

5. D: Since there are twice as many molecules of hydrogen present vs. oxygen, the partial pressure of hydrogen will be greater. The mass of hydrogen will not be greater than the mass of oxygen present even though there are more moles of hydrogen, due to oxygen having a higher molecular weight. Each gas will occupy the same volume. Hydrogen and oxygen gas can coexist in the container without reacting to produce water. There is no indication given that a chemical reaction has occurred.

6. C: Graham's law of diffusion allows one to calculate the relative diffusion rate between two different gases based on their masses.

7. D: London dispersion forces are the weakest intermolecular forces. These interactions occur in all molecules due to unequal electron density around the nucleus, which results in a momentary dipole. Dipole-dipole interactions are those between two polar molecules. The more positive portion of one molecule is attracted to the negative portion of a different molecule. Hydrogen bonding is a stronger type of dipole-dipole interaction which occurs between a hydrogen in one molecule and a nitrogen, oxygen or fluorine atom in another molecule. Hydrogen bonding only occurs between molecules containing H-F, H-O or H-N bonds. Ionic bonds are the strongest intermolecular forces. In ionic molecules, a positive ion is attracted to a negative ion. NaCl is entirely ionic with full charge separation, and the ions are tightly bound to each other in an organized crystalline network.

8. B: Plugging the data into the ideal gas law using the correct units gives the correct answer in atmospheres, which in this case is 2.4 atm. The equation is $P = nRT/V$. So we have $P = 1$ mol $(0.08206$ L atm/mol K$)(298$ K$)/10$ L. The R value is 0.08206 L atm/mol K when using L as the volume unit, and delivers the pressure in atm.

9. A: Since there are 7 moles of neon out of a total of 14 moles of gas in the cylinder, the partial pressure of neon will always be 50% of the total pressure, regardless of the temperature.

10. C: To convert from degrees Celsius to Kelvin, add 273. 75° C is equivalent to 348 K. Both X and Y have lower boiling points, which means that they will each boil in the water bath. Z will never become warm enough to boil.

11. D: Both liquids and gases are fluids and therefore flow, but only gases are compressible. The molecules that make up a gas are very far apart, allowing the gas to be compressed into a smaller volume.

12. C: The most electronegative atoms are found near the top right of the periodic table. Fluorine has a high electronegativity, while Cesium, located near the bottom left of the table, has a low electronegativity.

13. B: Since both the volume and the temperature remain fixed, the only variable that changes is the number of moles of particles. Because there are now 3 times the number of particles as there were originally, the pressure must increase proportionately and so the pressure must be 3 atm.

14. C: As the temperature drops to -5 °C, the water vapor condenses to a liquid, and then to a solid. The vapor pressure of a solid is much less than that of the corresponding gas. The argon is still a gas at -5 °C, so almost all the pressure in the cylinder is due to argon.

15. A: Heat is absorbed by the solid during melting, therefore ΔH is positive. Going from a solid to a liquid greatly increases the freedom of the particles, therefore increasing the entropy, so ΔS is also positive.

16. B: Freezing is an exothermic event; therefore heat must be given off. The temperature of the material remains unchanged at the freezing point during the process.

17. A: The higher the temperature of the liquid, the greater the solubility of the solid, while the higher the temperature, the lower the solubility of the gas.

18. C: Normality refers to the concentration of acid equivalents (H^+ ions), not the concentration of the solute. 100 g of phosphoric acid has a MW of 98 g/mol. So, 100g/98 g/mol = 1.02 moles of phosphoric acid are in solution. The total volume of the solution is 0.4 L, so the molarity of the solution is 1.02 mol/0.4 L = 2.55 M. Since there are three acid equivalents for every mole of phosphoric acid, the normality is 3 × 2.55 = 7.65 N.

19. D: $AgNO_3$, $NaNO_3$ and $NaCl$ are all highly water soluble and would not precipitate under these conditions. All nitrate compounds and compounds containing Group I metals are soluble in water. $AgCl$ is essentially insoluble in water, and this is the precipitate observed.

20. B: Density is determined by dividing the mass of the solution by its volume. The mass is 200 g, and the total volume is 0.2 L, or 200 mL. So 200 g/200 mL = 1 g/mL.

21. D: 100 mL of a 0.1 M solution of NaOH contains 0.01 moles of NaOH. That means 0.01 moles of acid are required to completely neutralize the solution. The MW of sulfuric acid is 98, so 0.98 g of sulfuric acid is 0.01 mole. But since sulfuric acid has two equivalents of acid per mole, only 0.005 mole of the acid is required or 0.49 g.

22. B: Pure water boils at 100 °C. Water that has salts dissolved in it will boil at a slightly higher temperature, and will conduct electricity much better than pure water.

23. D: Acidity increases as we travel down the periodic table with regard to the halogens. Even though fluorine is the most electronegative element and would be expected to stabilize a negative charge well, it is such a small atom that it is poorly able to stabilize the negative charge and therefore will have a stronger bond to the hydrogen. As the atoms get larger, moving from fluorine to iodine, the ability to stabilize a negative charge becomes greater and the bond with the hydrogen is weaker. A stronger bond with the between the halogen and the hydrogen will result in less acidity, since fewer hydrogen ions will be produced.

24. D: Octane is a nonpolar hydrocarbon with little or no water solubility. Butanol is an alcohol with a small amount of solubility due to its polar –OH group. Ethanol is a smaller, more polar alcohol that is very soluble in water. NaCl is an ionic salt that is highly soluble in water.

25. A: The weight % of the acetic acid is the mass of acetic acid divided by the mass of the acetic acid plus the water. So 50g/(50g +200g) = 0.2, or 20%. The mole fraction is the moles of acetic acid divided by the total number of moles of the solution. So 50 g of acetic acid (MW = 60) is 50g/ 60 g/mol = 0.83 moles. 200 g of water = 11.11 moles. Therefore, 0.83 mol/(0.83 mol + 11.11 mol) = 0.069.

26. C: Since there are three moles of NH_4^+ per mole of salt and 1 mole of PO_4^{3-} per mole of salt, the total ionic concentrations must be 2.7 M of NH_4^+, and 0.9 M of PO_4^{3-}.

27. B: Ethane is an alkane and only very weakly acidic. Methanol, an alcohol, has a slightly acidic proton attached to the oxygen. Acetic acid is much more acidic than methanol with the acidic proton attached to the carboxyl group. Hydrochloric acid is highly acidic and completely dissociates in water.

28. A: Since we have 1 liter of the solution, then 0.02 M represents 0.02 moles of methanol. The mass of methanol can then be found by 0.02mol × MW of CH_3OH (32) = 0.64 g. Molality is the moles of solute (methanol) divided by the number of kilograms of solvent, in this case, it is essentially 1 kg. This is assumed since the solvent is water and the density of water is 1 g/mL. So 0.02 mol/ 1 kg = 0.02 m.

29. D: During osmosis, solvent flows from the lowest to the highest concentration of solute, in this case B to A. The membrane is semi-permeable and only allows the solvent to move, not the solute.

30. B: Negative beta emission represents the spontaneous decay of a neutron into a proton with the release of an electron. Therefore the resulting nucleus will have one more proton than it did before the reaction, and protons represent the atomic number of an atom. Alpha decay results in the emission of a helium nucleus. The resulting nucleus of an alpha decay would lose two protons and two neutrons, causing a decrease in both the atomic number and the mass number. Gamma decay does not affect the numbers of protons or neutrons in the nucleus. It is an emission of a photon, or packet of energy.

31. C: Since each half life is 2 years, eight years would be 4 half lives. So the mass of material is halved 4 times. Therefore if we start with 1 kg, at two years we would have 0.5 kg, at four years we would have 0.25 kg, after 6 years we would have 0.12 kg, and after 8 years we would have 0.06 kg.

32. D: Using the decay formula, C-14 remaining = C-14 initial$(0.5)^{t/t\,half\text{-}life}$. So, 1 mg $(0.5)^{20000/5730}$ = 0.09 mg. This problem is best solved using the decay formula since 20,000 years is 3.5 half lives. If a student is careful in their reasoning, this problem can be solved without the decay formula. After 3 half-lives, there would be 0.125 mg remaining. If allowed to decay for 4 half-lives, 0.0625 mg would remain. Since only half of this half-life were allowed to elapse, only half of the material would decay, which would be 0.03 mg. Subtracting this amount from 0.125 mg, the amount remaining after 3 half-lives, gives 0.09 mg, which is the amount of material remaining after 3.5 half-lives.

33. D: Isotopes of the same element must have the same chemical behavior, so A, B, and C all represent, in one form or another, chemical behavior. Isotopes differ in mass, and this can be used to separate them by some appropriate physical property.

34. B: Neutrons are neutral in charge, and can impact a nucleus in order to break it.

35. A: Nuclear reactions convert mass into energy ($E = mc^2$). The mass of products is always less than that of the starting materials since some mass is now energy.

36. C: The mass number is the number of protons and the number of neutrons added together. The number of protons is also known as the atomic number and can be found on the periodic table. Therefore, the number of neutrons is the mass number (238) less the number of protons, in this case, 92, so we have 146 neutrons. The number of electrons always equals the number of protons in a neutral atom, so C is the correct answer.

37. D: An alpha particle is a helium nucleus, which contains two protons and two neutrons.

38. B: Phosphorus is in the third period, so the outermost levels must be 3s, 3p. Phosphorus is in Group 5A, which indicates that it has 5 valence electrons. To fill the 3s and 3p, 2 electrons first fill the s orbital, and then the remaining 3 electrons enter the p orbitals. So, $3s^2\ 3p^3$.

39. C: Hund's rule states that electrons must populate empty orbitals of similar energy before pairing up. The Aufbau principle states that electrons must fill lower energy orbitals before filling higher energy orbitals. The Pauli Exclusion Principle states that no two electrons in the same atom can have the same four quantum numbers, and therefore, two electrons in the same orbital will have opposite spins.

40. D: All of the elements belong to the same row in the periodic table. Atomic radii increase going from right to left in any row of the periodic table. Although these elements belonged to the same row, it is important to also know that atomic radii increase from top to bottom in the groups of the periodic table.

41. A: Sublimation is the process of a solid changing directly into a gas without entering the liquid phase. Fusion refers to a liquid turning into a solid. Diffusion is the process of a material dispersing throughout another. Condensation is generally a gas turning into a liquid.

42. D: Each oxygen has a charge of -2 for a total negative charge of -8. Potassium (K) only exists in compounds as +1. Therefore for the molecule to have a neutral charge, the Mn must be in a +7 oxidation state.

43. B: The trend within any column of the periodic table is that electronegativity decreases going down the column.

44. A: NaCl is an ionic salt, and therefore the most polar. F_2 is nonpolar since the two atoms share the electrons in an equal and symmetrical manner. CH_3OH is an alcohol with a very polar O-H bond. CH_3CH_2Cl is also a polar molecule due to the unequal sharing of electrons between in the C-Cl bond.

45. B: The nitrogen is missing its lone pair of electrons, and should have two dots above it. A correct Lewis structure shows how the atoms are connected to each other as well as all of the valence electrons in the compound. Each bond represents two electrons.

46. C: The more s character the bond has, the shorter it will be. A triple bond is stronger and shorter than a double bond, which is stronger and shorter than a single bond. An sp orbital is found in a triple bond. An sp^2 orbital is found in a double bond and sp^3 orbitals are found in single bonds.

47. D: Resonance structures have the same atoms connected to the same atoms, but differ only in electronic structure amongst the atoms. Isomers are molecules that have the same formula but differ in structure. Structural isomers differ in how the atoms are bonded to each other. Stereoisomers are isomers that have the same bonding structure but different arrangements, for example, cis- and trans- isomers.

48. B: Hybrid orbitals arrange themselves to be as far from each other as possible. An sp^2 atom has three hybrid orbitals, so they arrange themselves to be trigonal planar, with $120°$ between the bonds.

49. D: The correct structure of ammonium sulfate is $(NH_4)_2SO_4$. Its molecular weight is 132. The masses of the elements in the compound are: nitrogen 28 (2×14), hydrogen 8 (1×8), sulfur 32 (32×1) and oxygen 64 (16×4). To find the percentage composition of each element, divide the element mass by the molecular weight of the compound and multiply by 100. So nitrogen is ($28/132$) × 100 = 21%, hydrogen is ($8/132$) × 100 = 6%, sulfur is ($32/132$) × 100 = 24% and oxygen is ($64/132$) × 100 = 48%.

50. C: Three oxygen are equal to a total charge of -6. Therefore, the two iron atoms must equal that with a positive charge, or +6. So each iron atom must be +3, and the compound is iron (III) oxide.

51. A: By comparing the products to the reactants, there must be at least two Al atoms in the starting material, and at least three sulfate groups. Therefore, a coefficient of 2 must be placed in front of $Al(OH)_3$ and a coefficient of 3 must be placed in front of H_2SO_4. To make the number of hydrogen and oxygen atoms equal on both sides of the equation, a coefficient of 6 must be placed in front of H_2O.

52. D: 1 kg of heptane (MW 100) is equal to 10 moles of heptane. Since 8 moles of water is produced for every mole of heptane reacted, 80 moles of water must be produced. 80 moles of water (MW 18) equals 1440 g, or 1.4 kg.

53. C: 100 g of HBr equals 1.23 moles, and 100 g of Mg equals 4.11 moles. From the coefficients of the balanced equation, the ratio of HBr to Mg is 2:1. This means that to react 1.23 moles of HBr, 2.46 moles of Mg would be required. Since 4.11 moles of Mg are present, Mg is in excess.

54. C: The equation shows that for every liter of methane reacted, one liter of CO_2 and 2 liters of water vapor will be produced. So a total of three liters of gaseous products will be formed for every liter of methane burned. Because the temperature of the reaction products is 200 °C, the water produced will be in vapor (gas) form and not in liquid form. Since 10L of methane were burned, 30 L of gaseous products were formed.

55. B: Since the conversion of B to C is the slow step, this is the only one that determines the reaction rate law. Therefore, the rate law will be based on B, since it is the only reactant in producing C.

56. A: Since the atomic number is 20, which represents the number of protons in the atom, there must be an equal number of electrons in a neutral atom. Protons have a positive charge and electrons are negative. Equal numbers of protons and electrons will result in a neutral atom, or zero charge.

57. C: A pressure increase will force the reaction to go further to the right, which lowers gas pressure to restore equilibrium. Since the water formed is in the liquid phase, it does not appear in the equilibrium equation, so only 1 mole of gas is produced and is part of the equation.

58. D: For a general reaction, a A + b B→ c C + d D, the equilibrium equation would take the form:
$$K_{eq} = \frac{[C]^c[D]^d}{[A]^a[B]^b}$$
where a, b, c and d are the coefficients from the balanced chemical reaction. Pure liquids and solids are excluded from the equation. Since all reactants and products in the problem are gaseous, the equilibrium equation for the reaction would be:
$$K_{eq} = \frac{[CCl_4][HCl]^4}{[CH_4][Cl_2]^4}$$

59. C: Catalysts lower the energy barrier between products and reactants and thus increase the reaction rate.

60. D: 0.5 g of the salt dissolved, which is 0.005 mol of the salt. Since the volume is 1 L, the molarity of the salt is 0.005 M. This means that both species X and Y are present at 0.005 M concentration. The K_{sp} = [X][Y], or [0.005][0.005] which equals 2.5×10^{-5}.

61. A: Lewis acids are compounds capable of accepting a lone pair of electrons. $AlCl_3$ is a very strong Lewis acid and can readily accept a pair of electrons due to Al only having 6 electrons instead of 8 in its outer shell. $FeCl_3$ is also a strong Lewis acid, though milder than $AlCl_3$. Sulfuric acid is a Bronsted-Lowry acid since it produces protons. PCl_3 is a Lewis base since the P can donate its lone pair of electrons to another species.

62. B: NH_3 is ammonia, which is a base. H_2O is amphoteric, meaning that it can act as either a weak acid or a weak base. HF is actually a weak acid, despite fluorine being the most electronegative atom. The small size of the F results in a stronger bond between the H and F, which reduces acidity since this bond will be harder to break. H_3PO_4, phosphoric acid, is high in acidity and HCl is a very strong acid, meaning it completely dissociates.

63. A: First, one must understand that pK_a is the acidity dissociation number. The larger the number, the less acidic. Acetic acid is a carboxylic acid. When H^+ is given off, a negative charge results on the O. Because there is a second equivalent oxygen bonded to the same carbon, this negative charge can be shared between both oxygen atoms. This is known as resonance stabilization and this conjugate base will be more stable and more of the acid molecules will remain dissociated resulting in higher acidity. For ethanol, when the O-H bond breaks, the negative charge resides completely on the O. It cannot be stabilized by other atoms and therefore reforms the methanol rapidly. This results in very low acidity, since very few protons will be released.

64. C: HCl is a strong acid that will completely dissociate. pH = $-\log_{10}[H^+]$, which for this problem is pH=$-\log_{10}(0.1)$ = 1. The volume of the solution has no bearing on the pH since we know the concentration.

65. B: The K_a of acetic acid is determined from the pK_a, K_a = 10^{-pka} = 1.75×10^{-5}. This is the equilibrium constant for the acetic acid dissociation, or K_a = $[H^+][CH_3COO^-]/[CH_3COOH]$. Using this equilibrium equation to solve for the $[H^+]$, the pH of the buffer can then be found. Solving for the $[H^+]$ concentration, we get $[H^+]$ = $K_a \times [CH_3COOH]/CH_3COO^-]$, or $[H^+]$ = $1.75 \times 10^{-5} \times [0.1]/[0.2]$ = 8.75×10^{-6}. pH = $-\log[H^+]$ = 5.05.

66. C: There are 0.05 mol of sulfuric acid being added, but a total of 0.10 mol of H^+ since sulfuric acid is diprotic (H_2SO_4). This is being added to 0.1 mol of NaOH. The moles of acid and base exactly cancel each other out; therefore the pH of the resulting aqueous solution will be near 7.

67. D: To make a buffer, a weak acid and its conjugate base or a weak base and its conjugate acid are commonly used. Buffers work by using the common-ion effect and result in little change in the pH when an acid or a base is added. HCl/NaOH is a strong acid/strong base combination and will not result in a buffer solution. Although the $HNO_3/NaNO_3$ and $H_2SO_4/NaHSO_4$ mixtures are conjugate acid/base pairs, both HNO_3 and H_2SO_4 are strong acids, not weak acids. Neither of these solutions would result in a buffer. Only the

- 99 -

NaH_2PO_4/Na_2HPO_4 mixture would result in a buffer as it is a combination of a weak acid and its conjugate base.

68. A: When liquid water changes to steam, the temperature is constant, as in all phase changes. The entropy increases due to the increase in disorder from a liquid to a gas.

69. C: Cooling means heat is leaving the system, so it must be negative. We have 5.9 mol of ammonia cooling 75 °C, or 75 K. So 5.9 mol × -75 K × 35.1 J/(mol)(K) = -15.5 kJ.

70. A: The heat of combustion is determined by subtracting the heats of formation of the reactants from that of the products. So 3(-393.5) + 4(-285.8) – (-103.8) = -2220.
71. D: In I, dissolving a solid into a liquid breaks up the organized solid matrix, therefore increasing disorder. III converts single particles into two particles, and in IV, solid ice sublimes into a gas. Both of these processes also increase disorder and thus, entropy. II is a decrease in entropy, since 7 molecules, with 3 being gaseous, are reacted to form 2 solid molecules.

72. C: Because all unique materials have differing heat capacities, no two can heat up the same way. All will require different amounts of heat to warm to the same temperature.

73. D: Lead (Pb) goes from a zero oxidation state to a 2+ oxidation state, and is therefore oxidized. Oxidation is the loss of electrons. Hydrogen goes from a 1+ oxidation state to a 0 oxidation state, and is therefore reduced. Reduction is the gaining of electrons.

74. C: Reducing agents give up electrons to another chemical species, which cause that species to gain an electron and become reduced. Oxidizing agents cause another species to be oxidized, or to lose an electron, and are themselves reduced as they gain that electron. Bromine is very electronegative, and is almost always an oxidizing agent. N_2 is nearly inert, or unreactive. Neon is an inert noble gas and would not be a reducing agent. Sodium (Na) is very reactive and eager to give up an electron, and is therefore a good reducing agent in a wide variety of reactions.

75. C: Reduction takes place at the cathode and oxidation takes place at the anode. Mg^{2+} of the salt will be reduced to Mg(0) at the cathode, and Cl^- will be oxidized to Cl_2 at the anode.

76. D: The fact that ΔG for the reaction is negative indicates the reaction is spontaneous. This does not mean the reaction will be faster or slow. Diamonds as we all know do not rapidly convert to graphite, and in fact do so only very slowly, over millions of years, thank goodness.

77. A: The longest straight chain of carbons is four, so the parent name is butane. The alcohol takes number precedence, so it is in the -2- position, placing the methyl in the -3- position. The suffix becomes –ol since it is an alcohol, so the name is 3-methyl-2-butanol.

78. C: The first is an alkyne, which contains a triple bond between carbon atoms. The second is a ketone and contains a carbon-oxygen double bond. The third is an alkene, which has a double bond between two carbon atoms. The fourth is an imide, which contains a double bond between two nitrogen atoms.

79. B: The carbon of a carboxylic acid has three bonds to oxygen atoms and one to a carbon atom. The carbon bonded to the carboxylic carbon will have an oxidation state of zero. Each oxygen atom will have an oxidation number of -2. However, one oxygen is bonded to a hydrogen, which will have an oxidation number of +1. This results in a total oxidation state of -3 for both oxygens bonded to the carbon. Therefore, since the carbon must balance the oxidation states of the oxygens (-3) and the carbon (0), the oxidation state of the carbon must be +3. The three bonds to oxygen give a +3, and the bond to carbon is 0.

80. A: B is 1-butanol, since its longest chain of carbons is 4, not 3. C is 3-pentanone, since there are 5 carbons in the chain and it is a ketone, rather than a carboxylic acid. D is 1-butene, not 3-butene. The name should be assigned by giving the double bond the lowest number.

81. D: Mendeleev was able to connect the trends of the different elements behaviors and develop a table that showed the periodicity of the elements and their relationship to each other.

82. D: Different molecules must have the same chemical formula to be isomers. They differ only in which atoms are bound to which. Having the same molecular weight does not necessarily mean two molecules have the same formula.

83. B: Cis isomers have substituent groups that are on the same side of the molecule across the double bond. Trans isomers are those with substituent groups that are on opposite sides of the molecule across the double bond. I is neither cis nor trans, since both substituents on the same carbon are identical. IV is trans because the two methyl groups are on opposite sides of the molecule. II is cis due to both ethyl groups being on the same side of the molecule. III is also considered cis, although each substituent is different. The heaviest groups on each end of the double bond must be on the same side of the double bond to be cis.

84. A: NMR, or nuclear magnetic resonance, allows one to determine the connectivity of atoms in an organic molecule, by "reading" the resonance signals from the attached hydrogen atoms. IR, or infrared spectroscopy, can help to identify the functional groups that are present, but does not give much information about its position in the molecule. Mass spectrometry breaks apart a large molecule and analyzes the masses of the fragments. It can be useful in analyzing protein structure. HPLC, or high performance liquid chromatography, is a method used to separate a mixture into its components.

85. C: Proteins are large polypeptides, comprised of many amino acids linked together by an amide bond. DNA and RNA are made up of nucleic acids. Carbohydrates are long chains of sugars. Triglycerides are fats and are composed of a glycerol molecule and three fatty acids.

86. C: The closer the data points are to each other, the more precise the data. This does not mean the data is accurate, but that the results are very reproducible.

87. A: Density is mass per volume, typically expressed in units such as g/cm^3, or kg/m^3.

88. B: Acids and bases will react violently if accidentally mixed, as will reducing and oxidizing agents. Both reactions can be highly exothermic and uncontrollable.

89. A: Communities around the world who drink fluoridated water have shown dramatic decreases in the number of dental cavities formed per citizen versus those communities that do not drink fluoridated water.

90. D: Combustion of coal releases significant amounts of Hg into the atmosphere. When the Hg settles into the water, it becomes methylated and concentrates in fish, making them toxic to eat.

Secret Key #1 - Time is Your Greatest Enemy

Pace Yourself

Wear a watch. At the beginning of the test, check the time (or start a chronometer on your watch to count the minutes), and check the time after every few questions to make sure you are "on schedule."

If you are forced to speed up, do it efficiently. Usually one or more answer choices can be eliminated without too much difficulty. Above all, don't panic. Don't speed up and just begin guessing at random choices. By pacing yourself, and continually monitoring your progress against your watch, you will always know exactly how far ahead or behind you are with your available time. If you find that you are one minute behind on the test, don't skip one question without spending any time on it, just to catch back up. Take 15 fewer seconds on the next four questions, and after four questions you'll have caught back up. Once you catch back up, you can continue working each problem at your normal pace.

Furthermore, don't dwell on the problems that you were rushed on. If a problem was taking up too much time and you made a hurried guess, it must be difficult. The difficult questions are the ones you are most likely to miss anyway, so it isn't a big loss. It is better to end with more time than you need than to run out of time.

Lastly, sometimes it is beneficial to slow down if you are constantly getting ahead of time. You are always more likely to catch a careless mistake by working more slowly than quickly, and among very high-scoring test takers (those who are likely to have lots of time left over), careless errors affect the score more than mastery of material.

Secret Key #2 - Guessing is not Guesswork

You probably know that guessing is a good idea. Unlike other standardized tests, there is no penalty for getting a wrong answer. Even if you have no idea about a question, you still have a 20-25% chance of getting it right.

Most test takers do not understand the impact that proper guessing can have on their score. Unless you score extremely high, guessing will significantly contribute to your final score.

Monkeys Take the Test

What most test takers don't realize is that to insure that 20-25% chance, you have to guess randomly. If you put 20 monkeys in a room to take this test, assuming they answered once per question and behaved themselves, on average they would get 20-25% of the questions correct. Put 20 test takers in the room, and the average will be much lower among guessed questions. Why?
   1. The test writers intentionally write deceptive answer choices that "look" right. A test

taker has no idea about a question, so he picks the "best looking" answer, which is often wrong. The monkey has no idea what looks good and what doesn't, so it will consistently be right about 20-25% of the time.

2. Test takers will eliminate answer choices from the guessing pool based on a hunch or intuition. Simple but correct answers often get excluded, leaving a 0% chance of being correct. The monkey has no clue, and often gets lucky with the best choice.

This is why the process of elimination endorsed by most test courses is flawed and detrimental to your performance. Test takers don't guess; they make an ignorant stab in the dark that is usually worse than random.

$5 Challenge

Let me introduce one of the most valuable ideas of this course—the $5 challenge:

You only mark your "best guess" if you are willing to bet $5 on it.
You only eliminate choices from guessing if you are willing to bet $5 on it.

Why $5? Five dollars is an amount of money that is small yet not insignificant, and can really add up fast (20 questions could cost you $100). Likewise, each answer choice on one question of the test will have a small impact on your overall score, but it can really add up to a lot of points in the end.

The process of elimination IS valuable. The following shows your chance of guessing it right:

If you eliminate wrong answer choices until only this many remain:	Chance of getting it correct:
1	100%
2	50%
3	33%

However, if you accidentally eliminate the right answer or go on a hunch for an incorrect answer, your chances drop dramatically—to 0%. By guessing among all the answer choices, you are GUARANTEED to have a shot at the right answer.

That's why the $5 test is so valuable. If you give up the advantage and safety of a pure guess, it had better be worth the risk.

What we still haven't covered is how to be sure that whatever guess you make is truly random. Here's the easiest way:

Always pick the first answer choice among those remaining.

Such a technique means that you have decided, **before you see a single test question**, exactly how you are going to guess, and since the order of choices tells you nothing about which one is correct, this guessing technique is perfectly random.

This section is not meant to scare you away from making educated guesses or eliminating choices; you just need to define when a choice is worth eliminating. The $5 test, along with a pre-defined random guessing strategy, is the best way to make sure you reap all of the benefits of guessing.

Secret Key #3 - Practice Smarter, Not Harder

Many test takers delay the test preparation process because they dread the awful amounts of practice time they think necessary to succeed on the test. We have refined an effective method that will take you only a fraction of the time.

There are a number of "obstacles" in the path to success. Among these are answering questions, finishing in time, and mastering test-taking strategies. All must be executed on the day of the test at peak performance, or your score will suffer. The test is a mental marathon that has a large impact on your future.

Just like a marathon runner, it is important to work your way up to the full challenge. So first you just worry about questions, and then time, and finally strategy:

Success Strategy

1. Find a good source for practice tests.
2. If you are willing to make a larger time investment, consider using more than one study guide. Often the different approaches of multiple authors will help you "get" difficult concepts.
3. Take a practice test with no time constraints, with all study helps, "open book." Take your time with questions and focus on applying strategies.
4. Take a practice test with time constraints, with all guides, "open book."
5. Take a final practice test without open material and with time limits.

If you have time to take more practice tests, just repeat step 5. By gradually exposing yourself to the full rigors of the test environment, you will condition your mind to the stress of test day and maximize your success.

Secret Key #4 - Prepare, Don't Procrastinate

Let me state an obvious fact: if you take the test three times, you will probably get three different scores. This is due to the way you feel on test day, the level of preparedness you have, and the version of the test you see. Despite the test writers' claims to the contrary, some versions of the test WILL be easier for you than others.

Since your future depends so much on your score, you should maximize your chances of success. In order to maximize the likelihood of success, you've got to prepare in advance.

This means taking practice tests and spending time learning the information and test taking strategies you will need to succeed.

Never go take the actual test as a "practice" test, expecting that you can just take it again if you need to. Take all the practice tests you can on your own, but when you go to take the official test, be prepared, be focused, and do your best the first time!

Secret Key #5 - Test Yourself

Everyone knows that time is money. There is no need to spend too much of your time or too little of your time preparing for the test. You should only spend as much of your precious time preparing as is necessary for you to get the score you need.

Once you have taken a practice test under real conditions of time constraints, then you will know if you are ready for the test or not.

If you have scored extremely high the first time that you take the practice test, then there is not much point in spending countless hours studying. You are already there.

Benchmark your abilities by retaking practice tests and seeing how much you have improved. Once you consistently score high enough to guarantee success, then you are ready.

If you have scored well below where you need, then knuckle down and begin studying in earnest. Check your improvement regularly through the use of practice tests under real conditions. Above all, don't worry, panic, or give up. The key is perseverance!

Then, when you go to take the test, remain confident and remember how well you did on the practice tests. If you can score high enough on a practice test, then you can do the same on the real thing.

General Strategies

The most important thing you can do is to ignore your fears and jump into the test immediately. Do not be overwhelmed by any strange-sounding terms. You have to jump into the test like jumping into a pool—all at once is the easiest way.

Make Predictions

As you read and understand the question, try to guess what the answer will be. Remember that several of the answer choices are wrong, and once you begin reading them, your mind will immediately become cluttered with answer choices designed to throw you off. Your mind is typically the most focused immediately after you have read the question and digested its contents. If you can, try to predict what the correct answer will be. You may be surprised at what you can predict.

Quickly scan the choices and see if your prediction is in the listed answer choices. If it is, then you can be quite confident that you have the right answer. It still won't hurt to check the other answer choices, but most of the time, you've got it!

Answer the Question

It may seem obvious to only pick answer choices that answer the question, but the test writers can create some excellent answer choices that are wrong. Don't pick an answer just because it sounds right, or you believe it to be true. It MUST answer the question. Once you've made your selection, always go back and check it against the question and make sure that you didn't misread the question and that the answer choice does answer the question posed.

Benchmark

After you read the first answer choice, decide if you think it sounds correct or not. If it doesn't, move on to the next answer choice. If it does, mentally mark that answer choice. This doesn't mean that you've definitely selected it as your answer choice, it just means that it's the best you've seen thus far. Go ahead and read the next choice. If the next choice is worse than the one you've already selected, keep going to the next answer choice. If the next choice is better than the choice you've already selected, mentally mark the new answer choice as your best guess.

The first answer choice that you select becomes your standard. Every other answer choice must be benchmarked against that standard. That choice is correct until proven otherwise by another answer choice beating it out. Once you've decided that no other answer choice seems as good, do one final check to ensure that your answer choice answers the question posed.

Valid Information

Don't discount any of the information provided in the question. Every piece of information may be necessary to determine the correct answer. None of the information in the question is there to throw you off (while the answer choices will certainly have information to throw you off). If two seemingly unrelated topics are discussed, don't ignore either. You can be confident there is a relationship, or it wouldn't be included in the question, and you are probably going to have to determine what is that relationship to find the answer.

Avoid "Fact Traps"

Don't get distracted by a choice that is factually true. Your search is for the answer that answers the question. Stay focused and don't fall for an answer that is true but irrelevant. Always go back to the question and make sure you're choosing an answer that actually answers the question and is not just a true statement. An answer can be factually correct, but it MUST answer the question asked. Additionally, two answers can both be seemingly correct, so be sure to read all of the answer choices, and make sure that you get the one that BEST answers the question.

Milk the Question

Some of the questions may throw you completely off. They might deal with a subject you have not been exposed to, or one that you haven't reviewed in years. While your lack of knowledge about the subject will be a hindrance, the question itself can give you many clues that will help you find the correct answer. Read the question carefully and look for clues. Watch particularly for adjectives and nouns describing difficult terms or words that you don't recognize. Regardless of whether you completely understand a word or not, replacing it with a synonym, either provided or one you more familiar with, may help you to understand what the questions are asking. Rather than wracking your mind about specific detailed information concerning a difficult term or word, try to use mental substitutes that are easier to understand.

The Trap of Familiarity

Don't just choose a word because you recognize it. On difficult questions, you may not recognize a number of words in the answer choices. The test writers don't put "make-believe" words on the test, so don't think that just because you only recognize all the words in one answer choice that that answer choice must be correct. If you only recognize words in one answer choice, then focus on that one. Is it correct? Try your best to determine if it is correct. If it is, that's great. If not, eliminate it. Each word and answer choice you eliminate increases your chances of getting the question correct, even if you then have to guess among the unfamiliar choices.

Eliminate Answers

Eliminate choices as soon as you realize they are wrong. But be careful! Make sure you consider all of the possible answer choices. Just because one appears right, doesn't mean that the next one won't be even better! The test writers will usually put more than one good answer choice for every question, so read all of them. Don't worry if you are stuck between two that seem right. By getting down to just two remaining possible choices, your odds are now 50/50. Rather than wasting too much time, play the odds. You are guessing, but guessing wisely because you've been able to knock out some of the answer choices that you know are wrong. If you are eliminating choices and realize that the last answer choice you are left with is also obviously wrong, don't panic. Start over and consider each choice again. There may easily be something that you missed the first time and will realize on the second pass.

Tough Questions

If you are stumped on a problem or it appears too hard or too difficult, don't waste time. Move on! Remember though, if you can quickly check for obviously incorrect answer choices, your chances of guessing correctly are greatly improved. Before you completely give up, at least try to knock out a couple of possible answers. Eliminate what you can and then guess at the remaining answer choices before moving on.

Brainstorm

If you get stuck on a difficult question, spend a few seconds quickly brainstorming. Run through the complete list of possible answer choices. Look at each choice and ask yourself, "Could this answer the question satisfactorily?" Go through each answer choice and consider it independently of the others. By systematically going through all possibilities, you may find something that you would otherwise overlook. Remember though that when you get stuck, it's important to try to keep moving.

Read Carefully

Understand the problem. Read the question and answer choices carefully. Don't miss the question because you misread the terms. You have plenty of time to read each question thoroughly and make sure you understand what is being asked. Yet a happy medium must be attained, so don't waste too much time. You must read carefully, but efficiently.

Face Value

When in doubt, use common sense. Always accept the situation in the problem at face value. Don't read too much into it. These problems will not require you to make huge leaps of logic. The test writers aren't trying to throw you off with a cheap trick. If you have to go beyond creativity and make a leap of logic in order to have an answer choice answer the question, then you should look at the other answer choices. Don't overcomplicate the problem by creating theoretical relationships or explanations that will warp time or space. These are normal problems rooted in reality. It's just that the applicable relationship or explanation may not be readily apparent and you have to figure things out. Use your common sense to interpret anything that isn't clear.

Prefixes

If you're having trouble with a word in the question or answer choices, try dissecting it. Take advantage of every clue that the word might include. Prefixes and suffixes can be a huge help. Usually they allow you to determine a basic meaning. Pre- means before, post- means after, pro - is positive, de- is negative. From these prefixes and suffixes, you can get an idea of the general meaning of the word and try to put it into context. Beware though of any traps. Just because con- is the opposite of pro-, doesn't necessarily mean congress is the opposite of progress!

Hedge Phrases

Watch out for critical hedge phrases, led off with words such as "likely," "may," "can," "sometimes," "often," "almost," "mostly," "usually," "generally," "rarely," and "sometimes." Question writers insert these hedge phrases to cover every possibility. Often an answer choice will be wrong simply because it leaves no room for exception. Unless the situation calls for them, avoid answer choices that have definitive words like "exactly," and "always."

Switchback Words

Stay alert for "switchbacks." These are the words and phrases frequently used to alert you to shifts in thought. The most common switchback word is "but." Others include "although," "however," "nevertheless," "on the other hand," "even though," "while," "in spite of," "despite," and "regardless of."

New Information

Correct answer choices will rarely have completely new information included. Answer choices typically are straightforward reflections of the material asked about and will directly relate to the question. If a new piece of information is included in an answer choice that doesn't even seem to relate to the topic being asked about, then that answer choice is likely incorrect. All of the information needed to answer the question is usually provided for you in the question. You should not have to make guesses that are unsupported or choose answer choices that require unknown information that cannot be reasoned from what is given.

Time Management

On technical questions, don't get lost on the technical terms. Don't spend too much time on any one question. If you don't know what a term means, then odds are you aren't going to get much further since you don't have a dictionary. You should be able to immediately recognize whether or not you know a term. If you don't, work with the other clues that you have—the other answer choices and terms provided—but don't waste too much time trying to figure out a difficult term that you don't know.

Contextual Clues

Look for contextual clues. An answer can be right but not the correct answer. The contextual clues will help you find the answer that is most right and is correct. Understand the context in which a phrase or statement is made. This will help you make important distinctions.

Don't Panic

Panicking will not answer any questions for you; therefore, it isn't helpful. When you first see the question, if your mind goes blank, take a deep breath. Force yourself to mechanically go through the steps of solving the problem using the strategies you've learned.

Pace Yourself

Don't get clock fever. It's easy to be overwhelmed when you're looking at a page full of questions, your mind is full of random thoughts and feeling confused, and the clock is ticking down faster than you would like. Calm down and maintain the pace that you have set for yourself. As long as you are on track by monitoring your pace, you are guaranteed to have enough time for yourself. When you get to the last few minutes of the test, it may seem like you won't have enough time left, but if you only have as many questions as you should have left at that point, then you're right on track!

Answer Selection

The best way to pick an answer choice is to eliminate all of those that are wrong, until only one is left and confirm that is the correct answer. Sometimes though, an answer choice may immediately look right. Be careful! Take a second to make sure that the other choices are not equally obvious. Don't make a hasty mistake. There are only two times that you should stop before checking other answers. First is when you are positive that the answer choice you have selected is correct. Second is when time is almost out and you have to make a quick guess!

Check Your Work

Since you will probably not know every term listed and the answer to every question, it is important that you get credit for the ones that you do know. Don't miss any questions through careless mistakes. If at all possible, try to take a second to look back over your answer selection and make sure you've selected the correct answer choice and haven't made a costly careless mistake (such as marking an answer choice that you didn't mean to mark). The time it takes for this quick double check should more than pay for itself in caught mistakes.

Beware of Directly Quoted Answers

Sometimes an answer choice will repeat word for word a portion of the question or reference section. However, beware of such exact duplication. It may be a trap! More than likely, the correct choice will paraphrase or summarize a point, rather than being exactly the same wording.

Slang

Scientific sounding answers are better than slang ones. An answer choice that begins "To compare the outcomes..." is much more likely to be correct than one that begins "Because some people insisted..."

Extreme Statements

Avoid wild answers that throw out highly controversial ideas that are proclaimed as established fact. An answer choice that states the "process should used in certain situations, if..." is much more likely to be correct than one that states the "process should be discontinued completely." The first is a calm rational statement and doesn't even make a definitive, uncompromising stance, using a hedge word "if" to provide wiggle room, whereas the second choice is a radical idea and far more extreme.

Answer Choice Families

When you have two or more answer choices that are direct opposites or parallels, one of them is usually the correct answer. For instance, if one answer choice states "x increases" and another answer choice states "x decreases" or "y increases," then those two or three answer choices are very similar in construction and fall into the same family of answer choices. A family of answer choices consists of two or three answer choices, very similar in construction, but often with directly opposite meanings. Usually the correct answer choice will be in that family of answer choices. The "odd man out" or answer choice that doesn't seem to fit the parallel construction of the other answer choices is more likely to be incorrect.

Special Report: How to Overcome Test Anxiety

The very nature of tests caters to some level of anxiety, nervousness, or tension, just as we feel for any important event that occurs in our lives. A little bit of anxiety or nervousness can be a good thing. It helps us with motivation, and makes achievement just that much sweeter. However, too much anxiety can be a problem, especially if it hinders our ability to function and perform.

"Test anxiety," is the term that refers to the emotional reactions that some test-takers experience when faced with a test or exam. Having a fear of testing and exams is based upon a rational fear, since the test-taker's performance can shape the course of an academic career. Nevertheless, experiencing excessive fear of examinations will only interfere with the test-taker's ability to perform and chance to be successful.

There are a large variety of causes that can contribute to the development and sensation of test anxiety. These include, but are not limited to, lack of preparation and worrying about issues surrounding the test.

Lack of Preparation

Lack of preparation can be identified by the following behaviors or situations:

Not scheduling enough time to study, and therefore cramming the night before the test or exam
Managing time poorly, to create the sensation that there is not enough time to do everything
Failing to organize the text information in advance, so that the study material consists of the entire text and not simply the pertinent information
Poor overall studying habits

Worrying, on the other hand, can be related to both the test taker, or many other factors around him/her that will be affected by the results of the test. These include worrying about:

Previous performances on similar exams, or exams in general
How friends and other students are achieving
The negative consequences that will result from a poor grade or failure

There are three primary elements to test anxiety. Physical components, which involve the same typical bodily reactions as those to acute anxiety (to be discussed below). Emotional factors have to do with fear or panic. Mental or cognitive issues concerning attention spans and memory abilities.

Physical Signals

There are many different symptoms of test anxiety, and these are not limited to mental and emotional strain. Frequently there are a range of physical signals that will let a test taker know that he/she is suffering from test anxiety. These bodily changes can include the following:

Perspiring
Sweaty palms
Wet, trembling hands
Nausea
Dry mouth
A knot in the stomach
Headache
Faintness
Muscle tension
Aching shoulders, back and neck
Rapid heart beat
Feeling too hot/cold

To recognize the sensation of test anxiety, a test-taker should monitor him/herself for the following sensations:

The physical distress symptoms as listed above
Emotional sensitivity, expressing emotional feelings such as the need to cry or laugh too much, or a sensation of anger or helplessness
A decreased ability to think, causing the test-taker to blank out or have racing thoughts that are hard to organize or control.

Though most students will feel some level of anxiety when faced with a test or exam, the majority can cope with that anxiety and maintain it at a manageable level. However, those who cannot are faced with a very real and very serious condition, which can and should be controlled for the immeasurable benefit of this sufferer.

Naturally, these sensations lead to negative results for the testing experience. The most common effects of test anxiety have to do with nervousness and mental blocking.

Nervousness

Nervousness can appear in several different levels:

The test-taker's difficulty, or even inability to read and understand the questions on the test
The difficulty or inability to organize thoughts to a coherent form
The difficulty or inability to recall key words and concepts relating to the testing questions (especially essays)
The receipt of poor grades on a test, though the test material was well known by the test taker

Conversely, a person may also experience mental blocking, which involves:

Blanking out on test questions
Only remembering the correct answers to the questions when the test has already finished.

Fortunately for test anxiety sufferers, beating these feelings, to a large degree, has to do with proper preparation. When a test taker has a feeling of preparedness, then anxiety will be dramatically lessened.

The first step to resolving anxiety issues is to distinguish which of the two types of anxiety are being suffered. If the anxiety is a direct result of a lack of preparation, this should be considered a normal reaction, and the anxiety level (as opposed to the test results) shouldn't be anything to worry about. However, if, when adequately prepared, the test-taker still panics, blanks out, or seems to overreact, this is not a fully rational reaction. While this can be considered normal too, there are many ways to combat and overcome these effects.

Remember that anxiety cannot be entirely eliminated, however, there are ways to minimize it, to make the anxiety easier to manage. Preparation is one of the best ways to minimize test anxiety. Therefore the following techniques are wise in order to best fight off any anxiety that may want to build.

To begin with, try to avoid cramming before a test, whenever it is possible. By trying to memorize an entire term's worth of information in one day, you'll be shocking your system, and not giving yourself a very good chance to absorb the information. This is an easy path to anxiety, so for those who suffer from test anxiety, cramming should not even be considered an option.

Instead of cramming, work throughout the semester to combine all of the material which is presented throughout the semester, and work on it gradually as the course goes by, making sure to master the main concepts first, leaving minor details for a week or so before the test.

To study for the upcoming exam, be sure to pose questions that may be on the examination, to gauge the ability to answer them by integrating the ideas from your texts, notes and lectures, as well as any supplementary readings.

If it is truly impossible to cover all of the information that was covered in that particular term, concentrate on the most important portions, that can be covered very well. Learn these concepts as best as possible, so that when the test comes, a goal can be made to use these concepts as presentations of your knowledge.

In addition to study habits, changes in attitude are critical to beating a struggle with test anxiety. In fact, an improvement of the perspective over the entire test-taking experience can actually help a test taker to enjoy studying and therefore improve the overall experience. Be certain not to overemphasize the significance of the grade - know that the result of the test is neither a reflection of self worth, nor is it a measure of intelligence; one grade will not predict a person's future success.

To improve an overall testing outlook, the following steps should be tried:

Keeping in mind that the most reasonable expectation for taking a test is to expect to try to demonstrate as much of what you know as you possibly can.
Reminding ourselves that a test is only one test; this is not the only one, and there will be others.
The thought of thinking of oneself in an irrational, all-or-nothing term should be avoided at all costs.
A reward should be designated for after the test, so there's something to look forward to. Whether it be going to a movie, going out to eat, or simply visiting friends, schedule it in advance, and do it no matter what result is expected on the exam.

Test-takers should also keep in mind that the basics are some of the most important things, even beyond anti-anxiety techniques and studying. Never neglect the basic social, emotional and biological needs, in order to try to absorb information. In order to best achieve, these three factors must be held as just as important as the studying itself.

Study Steps

Remember the following important steps for studying:

Maintain healthy nutrition and exercise habits. Continue both your recreational activities and social pass times. These both contribute to your physical and emotional well being.
Be certain to get a good amount of sleep, especially the night before the test, because when you're overtired you are not able to perform to the best of your best ability.
Keep the studying pace to a moderate level by taking breaks when they are needed, and varying the work whenever possible, to keep the mind fresh instead of getting bored.
When enough studying has been done that all the material that can be learned has been learned, and the test taker is prepared for the test, stop studying and do something relaxing such as listening to music, watching a movie, or taking a warm bubble bath.

There are also many other techniques to minimize the uneasiness or apprehension that is experienced along with test anxiety before, during, or even after the examination. In fact, there are a great deal of things that can be done to stop anxiety from interfering with lifestyle and performance. Again, remember that anxiety will not be eliminated entirely, and it shouldn't be. Otherwise that "up" feeling for exams would not exist, and most of us depend on that sensation to perform better than usual. However, this anxiety has to be at a level that is manageable.

Of course, as we have just discussed, being prepared for the exam is half the battle right away. Attending all classes, finding out what knowledge will be expected on the exam, and knowing the exam schedules are easy steps to lowering anxiety. Keeping up with work will remove the need to cram, and efficient study habits will eliminate wasted time. Studying should be done in an ideal location for concentration, so that it is simple to become interested in the material and give it complete attention. A method such as SQ3R (Survey, Question, Read, Recite, Review) is a wonderful key to follow to make sure that the study habits are as effective as possible, especially in the case of learning from a textbook. Flashcards are great techniques for memorization. Learning to take good notes will mean that notes will be full of useful information, so that less sifting will need to be done to seek out what is pertinent for studying. Reviewing notes after class and then again on occasion will keep the information fresh in the mind. From notes that have been taken summary sheets and outlines can be made for simpler reviewing.

A study group can also be a very motivational and helpful place to study, as there will be a sharing of ideas, all of the minds can work together, to make sure that everyone understands, and the studying will be made more interesting because it will be a social occasion.

Basically, though, as long as the test-taker remains organized and self confident, with efficient study habits, less time will need to be spent studying, and higher grades will be achieved.

To become self confident, there are many useful steps. The first of these is "self talk." It has been shown through extensive research, that self-talk for students who suffer from test anxiety, should be well monitored, in order to make sure that it contributes to self confidence as opposed to sinking the student. Frequently the self talk of test-anxious students is negative or self-defeating, thinking that everyone else is smarter and faster, that they always mess up, and that if they don't do well, they'll fail the entire course. It is important to decreasing anxiety that awareness is made of self talk. Try writing any negative self thoughts and then disputing them with a positive statement instead. Begin self-encouragement as though it was a friend speaking. Repeat positive statements to help reprogram the mind to believing in successes instead of failures.

Helpful Techniques

Other extremely helpful techniques include:

Self-visualization of doing well and reaching goals
While aiming for an "A" level of understanding, don't try to "overprotect" by setting your expectations lower. This will only convince the mind to stop studying in order to meet the lower expectations.
Don't make comparisons with the results or habits of other students. These are individual factors, and different things work for different people, causing different results.
Strive to become an expert in learning what works well, and what can be done in order to improve. Consider collecting this data in a journal.
Create rewards for after studying instead of doing things before studying that will only turn into avoidance behaviors.
Make a practice of relaxing - by using methods such as progressive relaxation, self-hypnosis, guided imagery, etc - in order to make relaxation an automatic sensation.
Work on creating a state of relaxed concentration so that concentrating will take on the focus of the mind, so that none will be wasted on worrying.
Take good care of the physical self by eating well and getting enough sleep.
Plan in time for exercise and stick to this plan.

Beyond these techniques, there are other methods to be used before, during and after the test that will help the test-taker perform well in addition to overcoming anxiety.

Before the exam comes the academic preparation. This involves establishing a study schedule and beginning at least one week before the actual date of the test. By doing this, the anxiety of not having enough time to study for the test will be automatically eliminated. Moreover, this will make the studying a much more effective experience, ensuring that the learning will be an easier process. This relieves much undue pressure on the test-taker.

Summary sheets, note cards, and flash cards with the main concepts and examples of these main concepts should be prepared in advance of the actual studying time. A topic should never be eliminated from this process. By omitting a topic because it isn't expected to be on the test is only setting up the test-taker for anxiety should it actually appear on the exam. Utilize the course syllabus for laying out the topics that should be studied. Carefully go over the notes that were made in class, paying special attention to any of the issues that the professor took special care to emphasize while lecturing in class. In the textbooks, use the chapter review, or if possible, the chapter tests, to begin your review.

It may even be possible to ask the instructor what information will be covered on the exam, or what the format of the exam will be (for example, multiple choice, essay, free form, true-false). Additionally, see if it is possible to find out how many questions will be on the test. If a review sheet or sample test has been offered by the professor, make good use of it, above anything else, for the preparation for the test. Another great resource for getting to know the examination is reviewing tests from previous semesters. Use these tests to review, and aim to achieve a 100% score on each of the possible topics. With a few exceptions, the goal that you set for yourself is the highest one that you will reach.

Take all of the questions that were assigned as homework, and rework them to any other possible course material. The more problems reworked, the more skill and confidence will form as a result. When forming the solution to a problem, write out each of the steps. Don't simply do head work. By doing as many steps on paper as possible, much clarification and therefore confidence will be formed. Do this with as many homework problems as possible, before checking the answers. By checking the answer after each problem, a reinforcement will exist, that will not be on the exam. Study situations should be as exam-like as possible, to prime the test-taker's system for the experience. By waiting to check the answers at the end, a psychological advantage will be formed, to decrease the stress factor.

Another fantastic reason for not cramming is the avoidance of confusion in concepts, especially when it comes to mathematics. 8-10 hours of study will become one hundred percent more effective if it is spread out over a week or at least several days, instead of doing it all in one sitting. Recognize that the human brain requires time in order to assimilate new material, so frequent breaks and a span of study time over several days will be much more beneficial.

Additionally, don't study right up until the point of the exam. Studying should stop a minimum of one hour before the exam begins. This allows the brain to rest and put things in their proper order. This will also provide the time to become as relaxed as possible when going into the examination room. The test-taker will also have time to eat well and eat sensibly. Know that the brain needs food as much as the rest of the body. With enough food and enough sleep, as well as a relaxed attitude, the body and the mind are primed for success.

Avoid any anxious classmates who are talking about the exam. These students only spread anxiety, and are not worth sharing the anxious sentimentalities.

Before the test also involves creating a positive attitude, so mental preparation should also be a point of concentration. There are many keys to creating a positive attitude. Should fears become rushing in, make a visualization of taking the exam, doing well, and seeing an A written on the paper. Write out a list of affirmations that will bring a feeling of confidence, such as "I am doing well in my English class," "I studied well and know my material," "I enjoy this class." Even if the affirmations aren't believed at first, it sends a positive message to the subconscious which will result in an alteration of the overall belief system, which is the system that creates reality.

If a sensation of panic begins, work with the fear and imagine the very worst! Work through the entire scenario of not passing the test, failing the entire course, and dropping out of school, followed by not getting a job, and pushing a shopping cart through the dark alley where you'll live. This will place things into perspective! Then, practice deep breathing and create a visualization of the opposite situation - achieving an "A" on the exam, passing the entire course, receiving the degree at a graduation ceremony.

On the day of the test, there are many things to be done to ensure the best results, as well as the most calm outlook. The following stages are suggested in order to maximize test-taking potential:

Begin the examination day with a moderate breakfast, and avoid any coffee or beverages with caffeine if the test taker is prone to jitters. Even people who are used to managing caffeine can feel jittery or light-headed when it is taken on a test day.
Attempt to do something that is relaxing before the examination begins. As last minute cramming clouds the mastering of overall concepts, it is better to use this time to create a calming outlook.
Be certain to arrive at the test location well in advance, in order to provide time to select a location that is away from doors, windows and other distractions, as well as giving enough time to relax before the test begins.
Keep away from anxiety generating classmates who will upset the sensation of stability and relaxation that is being attempted before the exam.
Should the waiting period before the exam begins cause anxiety, create a self-distraction by reading a light magazine or something else that is relaxing and simple.

During the exam itself, read the entire exam from beginning to end, and find out how much time should be allotted to each individual problem. Once writing the exam, should more time be taken for a problem, it should be abandoned, in order to begin another problem. If there is time at the end, the unfinished problem can always be returned to and completed.

Read the instructions very carefully - twice - so that unpleasant surprises won't follow during or after the exam has ended.

When writing the exam, pretend that the situation is actually simply the completion of homework within a library, or at home. This will assist in forming a relaxed atmosphere, and will allow the brain extra focus for the complex thinking function.

Begin the exam with all of the questions with which the most confidence is felt. This will build the confidence level regarding the entire exam and will begin a quality momentum. This will also create encouragement for trying the problems where uncertainty resides.

Going with the "gut instinct" is always the way to go when solving a problem. Second guessing should be avoided at all costs. Have confidence in the ability to do well.

For essay questions, create an outline in advance that will keep the mind organized and make certain that all of the points are remembered. For multiple choice, read every answer, even if the correct one has been spotted - a better one may exist.

Continue at a pace that is reasonable and not rushed, in order to be able to work carefully. Provide enough time to go over the answers at the end, to check for small errors that can be corrected.

Should a feeling of panic begin, breathe deeply, and think of the feeling of the body releasing sand through its pores. Visualize a calm, peaceful place, and include all of the sights, sounds and sensations of this image. Continue the deep breathing, and take a few minutes to continue this with closed eyes. When all is well again, return to the test.

If a "blanking" occurs for a certain question, skip it and move on to the next question. There will be time to return to the other question later. Get everything done that can be done, first, to guarantee all the grades that can be compiled, and to build all of the confidence possible. Then return to the weaker questions to build the marks from there.

Remember, one's own reality can be created, so as long as the belief is there, success will follow. And remember: anxiety can happen later, right now, there's an exam to be written!

After the examination is complete, whether there is a feeling for a good grade or a bad grade, don't dwell on the exam, and be certain to follow through on the reward that was promised...and enjoy it! Don't dwell on any mistakes that have been made, as there is nothing that can be done at this point anyway.

Additionally, don't begin to study for the next test right away. Do something relaxing for a while, and let the mind relax and prepare itself to begin absorbing information again.

From the results of the exam - both the grade and the entire experience, be certain to learn from what has gone on. Perfect studying habits and work some more on confidence in order to make the next examination experience even better than the last one.

Learn to avoid places where openings occurred for laziness, procrastination and day dreaming.

Use the time between this exam and the next one to better learn to relax, even learning to relax on cue, so that any anxiety can be controlled during the next exam. Learn how to relax the body. Slouch in your chair if that helps. Tighten and then relax all of the different muscle groups, one group at a time, beginning with the feet and then working all the way up to the neck and face. This will ultimately relax the muscles more than they were to begin with. Learn how to breathe deeply and comfortably, and focus on this breathing going in and out as a relaxing thought. With every exhale, repeat the word "relax."

As common as test anxiety is, it is very possible to overcome it. Make yourself one of the test-takers who overcome this frustrating hindrance.

Additional Bonus Material

Due to our efforts to try to keep this book to a manageable length, we've created a link that will give you access to all of your additional bonus material.

Please visit http://www.mometrix.com/bonus948/ibchemistry to access the information.